# Lutheranism 101
# HOLY BAPTISM

Written by
Charles R. Lehmann

General Editor
Scot A. Kinnaman



CONCORDIA PUBLISHING HOUSE · SAINT LOUIS

## Lutheranism 101 Books

Lutheranism 101
Lutheranism 101: **THE COURSE**
Lutheranism 101: **FOR KIDS**
Lutheranism 101: **THE LORD'S SUPPER**
Lutheranism 101: **HOLY BAPTISM**
Lutheranism 101: **WORSHIP** *(forthcoming*


3558 S. Jefferson Ave., St. Louis, MO 63118-3968
1-800-325-3040 • www.cph.org



Manufactured in the United States of America

Library of Congress Cataloging-in-Publication Data
Lehmann, Charles R.
Lutheranism 101 : holy baptism / written by Charles R. Lehmann.
p. cm. – (Lutheranism 101 books)
ISBN 978-0-7586-3408-5
1. Baptism–Lutheran Church. 2. Baptism–Biblical teaching. I. Title. II. Title: Holy baptism.
BV811.3.L33 2013
234'.161–dc23
2012037622

5 6 7 8 9 10    29 28 27 26 25 24

# Contents

## Part Four: What Does Baptism Mean for Me Now?



## Appendix:



*Visit lutheranism101.com to download the free Leader Guide.*

# Foreword

*Lutheranism 101* books give you usable and comprehensive overviews of what Lutherans believe and teach. These beliefs rest upon the foundational discussions of who God is, who man is, and who Jesus is. Along the way, and because faith does not happen in isolation, the series also presents how this faith is confessed in what Lutherans do, both in their corporate practice and in their personal piety.

After the release of the original *Lutheranism 101* book, numerous questions, comments, and suggestions were received, focusing on the meeting point between faith and practice. The *Lutheranism 101* series grew out of this correspondence. Each book in the series picks one topic and explores the basics of the Lutheran teaching in that area. The author also explores practice in that area, the understanding being that one necessarily informs the other.

The very title, *Lutheranism 101*, points forward to the learning and building up of the Christian faith through study and by participation in the Divine Service. *Lutheranism 101* encourages the use (and, dare we say, acquisition) of the basic resources for a Christian's study and growth: a Bible, Luther's Small Catechism, a hymnal, and, ultimately, the Lutheran Confessions.

What Lutherans believe and teach about Baptism is different from what many other Christians teach. For Lutherans, Baptism is not a mere symbol of rebirth. It is not a choice or a prize for attaining a certain amount of faith. Most of all, it is how God bestows faith, cleanses sin, and makes us His family. It is for everyone, the very young to the very old. *Lutheranism 101: Baptism* gives an overview of what Baptism is, what it does, how it does it, and what it means for our lives now and into the future. Throughout, it emphasizes that the One doing the baptizing makes all the difference. Like the original book, *Lutheranism 101: Baptism* will never get too far away from the reality that it is all about Jesus.

Each chapter concludes with several questions that can be used to further the study and the discussion about the material. For those who may be leading a group discussion based upon the chapter, and for those individuals who want to check their answers against the author's comments, a free downloadable guide is available online at lutheranism101.com.

# Introduction

## More than Meets the Eye

Baptism is an extremely simple ritual. You pour water on a person or dunk the person in a pool, a lake, or a river. You say about twenty words. That's it. The whole thing is done in a few seconds. What is there to write about, really?

If that were all there is to Baptism, there wouldn't be much to say. In terms of what we do, Baptism isn't that complicated, and within a few minutes, even the water has evaporated. But that's the rub. The reason most American Christians don't think much about Baptism is that they really do think it's something *we do*. They see it as a simple act of obedience to God, as something a person does to show that he or she is a Christian.

But if we reduce Baptism to a mere human act, we miss almost everything that the Bible says about Baptism! Baptism is far more than something that we do to show God how much we love Him. Rather, Baptism is something *God does* to show how much He loves us. It is something He does to connect us sinners to the cross and resurrection of His Son and to give us the blessings won there.

## Knowing Who's Doing What

Keeping the order straight is one of the things we'll spend the most time on in this book. When Baptism is something that God does for us, then everything is different. When the Lord Himself is doing it, Baptism ceases to be a mere act of obedience and becomes a gracious gift of God.

**FROM THE BIBLE**

God shows His love for us in that while we were still sinners, Christ died for us. Since, therefore, we have now been justified by His blood, much more shall we be saved by Him from the wrath of God. (Romans 5:8–9)

**BELIEVE, TEACH, CONFESS**

To be baptized in God's name is to be baptized not by men, but by God Himself. Therefore, although it is performed by human hands, it is still truly God's own work. From this fact everyone may readily conclude that Baptism is a far higher work than any work performed by a man or a saint. For what work can we do that is greater than God's work? (LC IV 10)

That is why this book exists. Because Baptism is indeed something that God does, the Scriptures have a great deal to say about it. Because Baptism is something that God does, there is much comfort you can draw from knowing that God has done it for you. Because Baptism is something that God does, you've got an awful lot to rejoice about.

## Unbreakable Promises

In your Baptism, God has made promises to you that He can never break. It would be easier for God to destroy the very foundations of the earth than it would be for Him to take back the gifts that He gave in your Baptism. He would melt away a thousand galaxies, snuff out the sun, or undo the laws of physics before He would say that one whom He has baptized is not His precious and dearly beloved child.

That, dear Christian friends, is the Word that God has to say to you in your Baptism. He says it to you every day. He has claimed you through water in the Spirit. He loves you.

## A Sure and Certain Reality

Over the course of the next eight chapters, we are going to touch on all that the Scriptures say about Baptism. We won't be able to explore everything the Bible says in great detail. Instead, we'll develop the tools you'll need to continue your own study of the Scriptures. Along the way, we'll discover how the Scriptures speak of Baptism in the Old and New Testaments. We'll notice things about this wonderful gift that you've probably never noticed before.

We'll even begin to think of our own Baptism as a sure and certain reality that is present for us now and is not just a historical event in a past that we don't even remember.

**BELIEVE, TEACH, CONFESS**

What benefits does Baptism give?

It works forgiveness of sins, rescues from death and the devil, and gives eternal salvation to all who believe this, as the words and promises of God declare. (SC IV)

**WHAT DOES THIS MEAN?**

All that mortal
eye beholds
Is water as we pour it.
Before the eye of faith
unfolds
The pow'r of Jesus' merit.
For here it sees the crimson
flood
To all our ills bring healing;
The wonders of His precious
blood
The love of God revealing,
Assuring His own pardon.
(*LSB* 406:7)

# Abbreviations

| | |
|---|---|
| AE | Luther, Martin. *Luther's Works.* American Edition. Volumes 1–30: Edited by Jaroslav Pelikan. St. Louis: Concordia, 1955–76. Volumes 31–55: Edited by Helmut Lehmann. Philadelphia/Minneapolis: Muhlenberg/Fortress, 1957–86. Volumes 56–75: Edited by Christopher Boyd Brown. St. Louis: Concordia, 2009–. |
| Fast and Fast | Fast, Thomas E., and Fast, Carla H. *The Baptism of Your Child.* St. Louis: Concordia, 2007. |
| *LSB* | *Lutheran Service Book.* St. Louis: Concordia, 2006. |
| *Lutheranism 101* | Kinnaman, Scot A., gen. ed. *Lutheranism 101.* St. Louis: Concordia, 2010. |
| *LW* | *Lutheran Worship.* St. Louis: Concordia, 1982. |
| Scaer | Scaer, David P. *Baptism.* Vol. XI. Confessional Lutheran Dogmatics Series. Cresbard, South Dakota: Luther Academy, 1999. |
| *TLSB* | *The Lutheran Study Bible.* St. Louis: Concordia, 2009. |
| *WLS* | Plass, Ewald M., comp., *What Luther Says: A Practical In-Home Anthology for the Active Christian.* St. Louis: Concordia, 1959. |

## Lutheran Confessions

You will see many quotations from the Lutheran Confessions as found in the Book of Concord. The following list provides abbreviations used, what they mean, and examples of how you would find the text.

| | |
|---|---|
| AC | Augsburg Confession |
| Ap | Apology of the Augsburg Confession |
| BEC | A Brief Exhortation to Confession |
| Ep | Epitome of the Formula of Concord |
| FC | Formula of Concord |
| LC | Large Catechism |
| SA | Smalcald Articles |
| SC | Small Catechism |
| SD | Solid Declaration of the Formula of Concord |
| Tr | Treatise on the Power and Primacy of the Pope |

## Examples:

| | |
|---|---|
| AC XX 4 | (Augsburg Confession, Article XX, paragraph 4) |
| Ap IV 229 | (Apology of the AC, Article IV, paragraph 229) |
| FC SD X 24 | (Solid Declaration of the Formula of Concord, Article X, paragraph 24) |
| FC Ep V 8 | (Epitome of the Formula of Concord, Article V, paragraph 8) |
| LC V 32, 37 | (Large Catechism, Part 5, paragraphs 32 and 37) |
| SA III I 6 | (Smalcald Articles, Part III, Article I, paragraph 6) |
| SC III 5 | (Small Catechism, Part III, paragraph 5) |
| Tr 5 | (Treatise on the Power and Primacy of the Pope, paragraph 5) |

# Navigating Lutheranism 101

**WHAT DOES THIS MEAN?**
Quotes from Martin Luther

**MAKING CONNECTIONS**
Connecting theology, faith, and life

**NEED TO KNOW**
Terms and phrases quickly defined

**FROM THE BIBLE**
Quotations from, well, the Bible

**TECHNICAL STUFF**
Big theological concepts in bite-size pieces

**BELIEVE, TEACH, CONFESS**
Quotations from the Lutheran Confessions

# PART ONE

## What you'll learn about:

- We can never cleanse ourselves of sin, but God can and does through Baptism.
- Through water combined with His Word, God puts His holy name upon us and claims us as His family.
- God wants everyone to be baptized, including infants and the infirm.
- There are no conditions for belief or worthiness in order to be baptized.
- Baptism is commanded by Christ as a means of making disciples and may come before or after instruction in the faith.
- Baptism is the ordinary means by which we enter God's kingdom.

# What Is Baptism?

Water and God's Word—surely that can't be all there is to it! Yet, in such a simple way, God provides us with faith, new life, and a place in His family. What is Baptism? It's a mystery hidden right before our eyes. It's a washing that goes soul deep. It's our invitation and introduction into God's kingdom.

CHAPTER 1

# A Gift Instituted by Christ Himself

## In This Chapter

- Sin makes us so dirty that we can never clean ourselves.
- Baptism is a sacred washing through which God cleanses us of our sins.
- Baptism is water combined with God's Word.
- In Baptism, God's triune name is put upon us, giving us access to Him.

## Making Water "Cooler"

*Baptism* isn't a word that you hear much about when you're standing around the water cooler. It isn't a regular feature on the nightly news. It doesn't show up often on the *New York Times* best seller list. While most people have probably heard of it, many have only a very basic understanding of what it is.

For most, if they know anything about Baptism, they know this: Baptism is a Church ritual. Sometimes it happens in the church building at a special place with a bowl of water. Sometimes it happens outside in a river or a lake. Sometimes the person being baptized is a baby, and sometimes the person is much older. Baptism involves water and some words. That's about it. If you ask an unchurched person about Baptism, you probably won't hear much more than this.

But that's really a pretty good start. Baptism *is* a Church ritual that involves water and words. Sometimes just a little water is used, and sometimes a lot is used. Baptism can happen in a variety of locations. And, finally, a person can be baptized at any age. All of these things are true.

Despite that, the most important questions still haven't been answered.

What's the point?

Why get wet in the first place?

What good is it?

The answers to those questions are what will occupy most of our time.

## Splish! Splash!

One of the most fundamental things we can say about Baptism is that it's a bath. The original languages in which the Bible was written give even more insights into this. Most of the Old Testament was written in Hebrew, and the New Testament was written in Greek. The Greek word for *Baptism* means "bath"—in other words, washing. This is important. Most people take baths for a reason, for a specific purpose. Dirty people take baths to get clean.

That's also why people are baptized. All people are born dirty. All people need to get clean. Most important, God wants them to be clean. He says it outright through His prophet Ezekiel: "I will sprinkle clean water on you, and you shall be clean from all your uncleannesses, and from all your idols I will cleanse you. And I will give you a new heart, and a new spirit I will put within you. And I will remove the heart of stone from your flesh and give you a heart of flesh. And I will put My Spirit within you, and cause you to walk in My statutes and be careful to obey My rules" (Ezekiel 36:25–27).

So let's get to it. How are we dirty, and what does Baptism do about it?

### Dirty as Sin

If you've ever seen a baby seconds after he or she was born, you know why people don't usually take the picture right away. The baby is covered in blood and tissue from the birth process. While beautiful to his or her parents, the child is most definitely *not* clean. A nurse wipes the baby off almost immediately, and within the first few hours of life outside the womb, the newborn gets a bath.

But as filthy as the baby looks at the time of birth, his or her spiritual condition is even worse. The baby is completely soiled with sin. It sounds weird to say that babies are sinners, but that's just what the Bible says. In fact, babies are sinners even before they're born. They are sinful from the moment they are conceived, for sin is an inherited condition. David writes, "Behold, I was brought forth in iniquity, and in sin did my mother conceive me" (Psalm 51:5). Adam and Eve were created in the image and likeness of God (Genesis 1:26–28). God created them holy because He wanted to be in a perfect relationship with them. Everything

**TECHNICAL STUFF**

Sin is the condition of humanity that completely separates us from God. It is every bad thing we think, say, or do. Even worse, our sinful nature compels us to think, say, and do only what is wrong. We inherited it from the first human beings, Adam and Eve, who separated themselves from God by disobeying His command in the Garden of Eden.

changed after Adam's sin. Adam lost the perfect holiness and innocence he originally had, and because of that, he passed on his sin instead of the perfect righteousness he had in the beginning. Ever since the fall, all human beings have been conceived and born in the sinful image of their fathers (Genesis 5:3; Romans 5:12).

## Grime Time

Sin is serious stuff, and we're all affected by it. It's dirt that we can't get rid of on our own. I once knew a man who worked in a steel plant. For hours on end, he worked in areas coated with soot, grime, and pulverized coal dust. When he came home, he would wash himself thoroughly, but it was never enough. You could always find the grime somewhere—in his hair, under his fingernails, and in the wrinkles of his skin. He couldn't get rid of it any more than he could get rid of a finger or an eye. That's what sin is like. In fact, references to dirt and filth are some of the Bible's favorite ways of talking about it! In Psalm 51:2, David prays, "Wash me thoroughly from my iniquity, and cleanse me from my sin!" Later he says, "Purge me with hyssop, and I shall be clean; wash me, and I shall be whiter than snow" (v. 7).

David's thoughts about his sin are pretty clear. Sin made David dirty, and he couldn't wash himself. The reason that we must be washed is that sin puts us in complete opposition to God. It cuts us off from full reception of His presence, His gifts, and His goodness. We have neither the desire nor the ability to rescue ourselves from our sinful condition. We are, in fact, dead, as Paul puts it: "And you were dead in the trespasses and sins in which you once walked, following the course of this world, following the prince of the power of the air, the spirit that is now at work in the sons of disobedience—among whom we all once lived in the passions of our flesh, carrying out the desires of the body and the mind, and were by nature children of wrath, like the rest of mankind" (Ephesians 2:1–3).

**FROM THE BIBLE**

Though you wash yourself with lye and use much soap, the stain of your guilt is still before Me, declares the Lord God. (Jeremiah 2:22)

## More Than Skin Deep

In his novel *The Voyage of the Dawn Treader*, C. S. Lewis tells the story of Eustace, a boy who becomes a dragon because of his greed. Eventually, Eustace is desperate to shed his dragon skin and become a boy again. He claws at his skin over and over, but he learns that no matter how many times he sheds his dragon skin, he's still a dragon underneath. Eustace needs Aslan to remove the dragon skin for him. Fortunately, Aslan—the lion who serves as a Christ figure—is waiting to help him. After he removes Eustace's scales, Aslan heals Eustace by sending him into—you guessed it—a bath.

Lewis loved to weave Christian theological themes into his stories. It's no surprise at all that Baptism has a role to play in Narnia. Unless Aslan washes Eustace, the boy will never be clean. Unless we are washed, we will never be clean either.

## Water and Word

### A Special Word

Baptism is unique because it is a holy washing, a spiritual bath that cleanses us from sin. We don't get out of our bathtubs each morning and say, "I just baptized myself." For starters, Baptism is something done to us, not something we do to ourselves. More to the point, there is something special and unique about Baptism that sets it apart from an ordinary bath. If there wasn't, then we could just use the word any time we wanted to refer to any sort of bathing. *Baptism* is a special word; it is used almost exclusively by the Church.

The term the Church uses for Baptism is *sacrament*, and whenever the Church talks about a sacrament, it does so on the basis of what Jesus says when He first institutes it. The word *sacrament* is used by the Church to refer to several specific ways that God has promised to deliver the forgiveness of sins, life, and salvation to His people.

The Lord's Supper: the Sacrament in which the forgiveness of sins is delivered by the eating of Jesus' body and the drinking of His blood in, with, and under the elements of bread and wine.

**FROM THE BIBLE**

*Baptism* is a good example of theological jargon. We will discuss many other theological words in this book, including some that Lutherans define in unique ways. When a word of theological jargon is first used, it will often be accompanied by a "Need to Know" box in the margin.

**MAKING CONNECTIONS**

One of the few times the secular world uses the word ***baptism*** is in the phrase ***baptism by fire***, referring to a difficult initiation into a new job or other situation. It means to do something the hard way. Our Baptism in the Church is not this way at all. It is not a test of our abilities, and it is not hard. God acts, and we receive all the benefits of a "position" in His family.

**NEED TO KNOW**

**Sacrament:** from the Greek word meaning "mystery"; literally, "something sacred." In the Lutheran Church, a Sacrament is a sacred act that (1) was instituted by God, (2) has a visible element, and (3) offers the forgiveness of sins earned by Christ. The Sacraments include Baptism, the Lord's Supper, and also Absolution (if one counts the pastor as the visible element [LC IV 74; Ap XIII 4–5]).

**TECHNICAL STUFF**

While most Scripture in this book is from the English Standard Version (ESV), a few key passages are from the 1984 edition of the New International Version (NIV) to match the current catechism edition. In some cases, the author uses his own translation to show something that is clear in the original language but is less clear in the currently available translations of the Scriptures. In the case of Matthew 28:19, the participles "baptizing" and "teaching" modify the verb "make disciples." By supplying the word "by," the relationship between the participles and the main verb is clarified.

Holy Absolution: the Sacrament in which a pastor forgives sins (often very specific) that are confessed to him either privately or within a worship service.

When you hear "promise of grace," you should think "forgiveness of sins." Baptism is a sacrament because God commands it and because through it, God actually does wash away—forgive—our sins. To say that Baptism is a sacrament is a wonderful thing. It tells us something about the fantastic blessings that God has in store for us through it.

## Not Just a Ducky

So what distinguishes Christian Baptism from what happens when you're in the bathtub with your rubber ducky? There is no better place to find the answer than the Scripture passage in which Jesus gives us the gift of Baptism. Shortly before His ascension, Jesus tells His apostles to "make disciples of all nations by baptizing them into the name of the Father, the Son, and the Holy Spirit" (Matthew 28:19, author's translation).

From our Lord's words we learn that two things must be present in order for a bath to be a Baptism: water and God's Word. Though water is not explicitly mentioned in our Lord's words, it is certainly there. Water is implied by the word "baptize." To baptize is to wash with water. If there is no water, there is no Baptism. What makes the bath of Baptism different from any other bath is that the water is combined with God's Word.

When a person is baptized, the words that are used are those that Christ used when He instituted Baptism: "I baptize you in the name of the Father and of the Son and of the Holy Spirit" (*LSB*, p. 270). Water and the Word together are what make an ordinary bath a Christian Baptism.

## Stopping for Water

A story from just a few years after our Lord instituted Baptism illustrates this point. At that time, the Christian Church was growing so much that the apostles found they needed extra help. Because of this, they appointed seven men to assist them in their work of proclaiming God's Word. One of these men, named Philip, was sent to speak to a eunuch as he was traveling.

The eunuch was going home to Ethiopia, where he served in the court of Queen Candace. As he traveled, he read a passage from Isaiah's prophecy about Jesus' suffering, death, and resurrection: "Like a sheep He was led to the slaughter and like a lamb before its shearer is silent, so He opens not His mouth. In His humiliation justice was denied Him. Who can describe His generation? For His life is taken away from the earth" (Acts 8:32–33, quoting Isaiah 53:7–8). When Philip arrived, he asked the eunuch if he understood what he was reading. The eunuch answered that there was no way he could understand it unless someone explained it to him.

Luke continues the story with these words: "Then Philip opened his mouth, and beginning with this Scripture he told him the good news about Jesus. And as they were going along the road they came to some water, and the

**TECHNICAL STUFF**

Unless your Bible is the King James or New King James Version, you may notice that verse 37 is missing. That is because the manuscript used when the verse numbers were assigned included a few verses that were probably added by scribes several hundred years after the Bible was written. The earliest and best manuscripts don't have these verses.

**MAKING CONNECTIONS**

The Jordan is a 156-mile river that forms the eastern border of the modern nation of Israel (and of the occupied territories). It begins 60 miles north of the Sea of Galilee and ends in the Dead Sea. In biblical history, the Jordan was very prominent. The Israelites formally entered the land God had promised to them when they crossed the Jordan after forty years of wilderness wanderings. Later, Naaman the Syrian was cleansed of his leprosy by washing in the Jordan. At the beginning of His ministry, Jesus was baptized by John in the Jordan River.

eunuch said, 'See, here is water! What prevents me from being baptized?' . . . And he commanded the chariot to stop, and they both went down into the water, Philip and the eunuch, and he baptized him" (Acts 8:35–36, 38).

Luke's account in Acts 8 gives us a glimpse into the simplicity of Baptism. All that the eunuch needed in order to be baptized was water and a person to perform the Baptism. Philip dunked him in the water, he spoke the Lord's words, and the eunuch was baptized. There was no need for the eunuch to travel to the Jordan River (where Jesus was baptized) or even to a nearby synagogue. The stream that they passed by in the chariot was completely sufficient.

## $SH_2O$+

The water of Baptism, however, is no ordinary water. Luther puts it this way: "Baptism is not just plain water, but it is the water included in God's command and combined with God's word" (SC IV, First). Luther knows how to pack a lot of theology into just a few words. Because of that, we need to unpack that sentence a bit.

When Luther says that Baptism is not plain water, he does not mean that it is not the chemical composed of two hydrogen atoms and one oxygen atom. He means that through the Word of God, the water has become something more than what it initially was.

## High Stakes Water

Luther describes it in the Large Catechism: "Baptism is quite a different thing from all other water. This is not because of its natural quality but because something more noble is added here. God Himself stakes His honor, His power, and His might on it. Therefore, Baptism is not only natural water, but a divine, heavenly, holy, and blessed water, and whatever other terms we can find to praise it.

**MAKING CONNECTIONS**

Because of its historic significance, some Christians purchase water from the Jordan to be used in their Baptisms. While there is nothing wrong with doing this, being baptized with Jordan River water doesn't convey any blessing that you would not receive through a Baptism that used tap water.

**FROM THE BIBLE**

"For as the rain and the snow come down from heaven and do not return there but water the earth, making it bring forth and sprout, giving seed to the sower and bread to the eater, so shall My word be that goes out from My mouth; it shall not return to Me empty, but it shall accomplish that which I purpose, and shall succeed in the thing for which I sent it." (Isaiah 55:10–11)

This is all because of the Word, which is a heavenly, holy Word, which no one can praise enough. For it has, and is able to do, all that God is and can do" (LC IV 17).

Luther says that the water is "included in God's command." The command is what Jesus says in Matthew 28:19: make disciples by baptizing. If the Lord hadn't commanded that we baptize, we could use exactly the same words that we use now, and they would have no effect. But because of the Lord's institution and mandate, the words do what they say.

Luther also notes that the water is "combined with God's Word." Even better, the Word of God that is combined with the water is nothing less than God's own name: Father, Son, and Holy Spirit (Matthew 28:19). When you are baptized, God's name is poured on you with the water. In the Bible, having God's name on you is a blessing.

## The Gift of God's Name

Since the Word of God that is combined with the water in Baptism is God's own name, it's important to pay special attention to what the Bible says about names in general and God's name in particular. Depending on how the Hebrew word for "name" is used in the Bible, it can mean a lot more than just a personal name, such as Tiger or Elizabeth. It can embody a person's whole reputation. If I say Tiger Woods or Elizabeth II, a lot is going to come to mind beyond the fact that these names refer to two particular people. When I say Tiger Woods, you will probably think both of his golf ability and of his extramarital affair. When I say Elizabeth II, you will probably remember her as the queen of the United Kingdom. In either case, there's a lot more to each of those names than just what's on the birth certificate.

**MAKING CONNECTIONS**

Our Lord speaks and we listen. His Word bestows what it says. Faith that is born from what is heard acknowledges the gifts received with eager thankfulness and praise. . . . Saying back to [God] what He has said to us, we repeat what is most true and sure. Most true and sure is His name, which He put upon us with the water of our Baptism. (*LW*, p. 6)

Some in the ancient world believed that if you knew the true name of a deity, you would have enormous power over that being. The way the Bible talks about God's name was unique. It was something the world had never encountered before.

Jesus' own words make it clear that in Baptism, God puts His name on *you*. It is God's triune name that is combined with the baptismal waters, and this is a glorious reality. Indeed, God has some amazing and important things to say about His name throughout the Scriptures.

**NEED TO KNOW**

**Yahweh:** The Hebrew language originally did not have vowels. God's name is written YHWH. However, we know how God's name is pronounced because of the way it is written when combined with other words like *Hallelujah* and because of the way it was transposed into Greek in the ancient world.

**MAKING CONNECTIONS**

Psalm 136 connects all of God's mighty acts of salvation in the Old Testament with His name. It begins in a way that summarizes the whole psalm: "Give thanks to the LORD, for He is good, for His steadfast love endures forever" (v. 1). Each successive verse praises God for who He is and what He has done for His people.

## An Unspeakably Good Name

God gives His name to us in a formal way for the first time in the Old Testament in Exodus 3. The name given there is "Yahweh." Just as "Father, Son, and Holy Spirit" is the way God is known in the New Testament, "Yahweh" is the name by which He is known in the Old Testament. But even though God gives us His personal name and it shows up nearly seven thousand times in the Old Testament alone, you will not see it written out in most translations. The custom among the Jews in the first century was to say the Hebrew word for "Lord" or "Master" whenever they saw "Yahweh" written in the Old Testament. The Jews thought that if they never said God's name, they would never misuse it.

Most translations follow this ancient custom. In them, God's name is rendered as "the LORD." When you see "LORD" printed in all capital letters, the word that actually appears in the Hebrew text of the Old Testament is "Yahweh." This is important for us to know as we explore the Old Testament passages that speak about God's name. It will help us better understand the relationship between God's name and Baptism. After God gives Moses His name in Exodus 3, we have this important verse: "God also said to Moses, 'Say this to the people of Israel, "The LORD, the God of your fathers, the God of Abraham, the God of Isaac, and the God of Jacob, has sent me to you." This is My name forever, and thus I am to be remembered throughout all generations' " (v. 15).

*Yahweh* is the name in the Old Testament that is intended to bring to mind all that God does for His people. Moses makes this clear by the way he tells the story. In the beginning of the Book of Exodus, Moses shares how Pharaoh was murdering all of Israel's baby boys. Moses is saved when his mother disobeys Pharaoh's command. In chapter 3, God calls Moses in the desert of Midian and sends him back to Egypt to save the Israelites from their slavery there. This is when God first gives His name in a formal way and discusses its importance. From this point on in Exodus, Moses says "Thus says the LORD" to Pharaoh eight times before Israel is finally set free. In the Old Testament, the name *Yahweh* is the name of the God who frees His people from bondage and death. When God puts His name on His people through Baptism, He is saying that all of the promises that He attaches to His name apply to the one who has been baptized.

## Proper Use of God's Name

Because God's name is so important, the second of the Ten Commandments is focused on guarding it against frivolous or blasphemous use. "You shall not take the name of the LORD your God in vain, for the LORD will not hold him guiltless who takes His name in vain" (Exodus 20:7). When God guards His name, He is also guarding His reputation and all those who bear His name through the waters of Holy Baptism.

Luther gives an explanation of the Second Commandment in the Small Catechism: "We should fear and love God so that we do not curse, swear, use satanic arts, lie, or deceive by His name, but call upon it in every trouble, pray, praise, and give thanks" (SC I).

Luther's central point is that God gives His name to us because He wants us to use it. He wants us to "call upon it in every trouble, pray, praise, and give thanks." These are all ways that the Israelites were given to use God's name during their deliverance from bondage in Egypt. At that time, God began to call the Israelites His children (Exodus 4:22). The language that Moses uses in the Book

**TECHNICAL STUFF**

At the burning bush, God identifies Himself using the name **Yahweh**, but this name is used throughout the Book of Genesis, starting with chapter 2, both in Moses' narration and when people talk about God. By giving Moses His name, God was identifying Himself as the one who had established a covenant with Abraham, Isaac, and Jacob.

**MAKING CONNECTIONS**

Through Baptism we are members of God's family. This theme is extremely common in the prayers of the Church. The Collect for Good Friday reads, *"Almighty God, graciously behold this Your family for whom our Lord Jesus Christ was willing to be betrayed and delivered into the hands of sinful men to suffer death upon the cross; through the same Jesus Christ, Your Son, our Lord, who lives and reigns with You and the Holy Spirit, one God, now and forever. Amen."* (L33) of Exodus makes it clear that Yahweh was not just the name of the God of the Israelites. Yahweh was a *family* name.

Luther echoes this idea when he talks about God's name again in his discussion of the Lord's Prayer. He writes, "God's name is kept holy when the Word of God is taught in its truth and purity, and we, as the children of God, also lead holy lives according to it" (SC III, First Petition).

For Luther, being baptized and being a child of God are the same thing. When God puts His name on us in the waters of Baptism, He is adopting us into His own family. As bearers of God's name, we are also bearers of God's reputation. What a Christian does reflects back upon God Himself.

## God Puts His Name on His People

God reveals His name to us in different ways in the Old and New Testaments. In the Old Testament, He gives His name as "Yahweh." In the New Testament, He gives His name as "Father, Son, and Holy Spirit." Baptism is the way that God promises to put His name on Christians in the New Testament, but there was also a unique way in which God put His name on His people in the Old Testament. The way God does this important work reveals much about Baptism.

**MAKING CONNECTIONS**

The Aaronic blessing used in the Divine Service gives God the last word: "The Lord bless you and keep you. The Lord make His face shine on you and be gracious to you. The Lord look upon you with favor and give you peace." (The Benediction. *LSB*, p. 166)

### The LORD

The Book of Numbers teaches that God wanted His people to bear His name. This was accomplished through the speaking of a particular blessing:

> The LORD spoke to Moses, saying, "Speak to Aaron and his sons, saying, Thus you shall bless the people of Israel: you shall say to them,
>
> The LORD bless you and keep you;
>
> the LORD make His face to shine upon you and be gracious to you;
>
> the LORD lift up His countenance upon you and give you peace.
>
> "So shall they put My name upon the people of Israel, and I will bless them." (Numbers 6:22–27)

The words of this blessing are very familiar. You've probably heard them in church more than once. The pastor speaks them at the end of the service, after everything else has happened. You've already confessed your sins and received forgiveness. You've already heard the Word of God read and proclaimed. You've already been given your Lord's body to eat and His blood to drink in the Lord's Supper.

Finally, at the end of the service, you hear these words: "The LORD . . . . The LORD . . . . The LORD . . . ." The personal name of God is spoken three times. Each time you hear God's name, He is doing something tremendous for you. First, He blesses you and keeps you. Then, His face shines upon you and He's gracious (forgiving) to you. Finally, He lets His face (countenance) shine upon you in favor, and He gives you peace (health, wholeness, well-being). Through this threefold giving of His name, God puts His "name upon the people of Israel" and He blesses you.

## The Name Is Enough

"Blessing" in the Bible means a showering of divine favor. Anytime God gives His people anything that is good, He is blessing them. When God tells Aaron to bless His people with these words, He says something very interesting: "So shall they put My name upon the people of Israel, and I will bless them" (Numbers 6:27).

What is the blessing? The name! The name is enough! It is actually impossible to think of a greater blessing than God putting His own name upon you. Isaiah fleshes this out a bit when he writes, "Fear not, for I have redeemed you; I have called you by name, you are Mine. . . . For I am the LORD your God, the Holy One of Israel, your Savior" (Isaiah 43:1, 3). In Baptism, God does this. He puts His name on us and calls us by it. He claims us as His very own.

I still remember the day I first learned to write my name. When I realized it was my name, nothing in the house was safe. I wrote my name anywhere and everywhere I could. The reason I was so excited was simple: I knew that if I put my name on something, I was claiming it as my own. You can see why it is such a blessing to have God's name on us. By putting His name on us, He claims us, and He promises to take our welfare seriously. The word "keep" in the Aaronic benediction could also be translated as "cherish." God cherishes us. He invests in us and makes us part of His family.

## Father, Son, and Holy Spirit

God commanded Aaron to put His name on His people in a threefold way. The consistent teaching of the Old Testament is that God is absolutely unified (Deuteronomy 6:4), and that within that unity, there is some sort of plurality. When God creates man, He says, "Let Us make man in Our image, after Our likeness" (Genesis 1:26).

**NEED TO KNOW**

**Trinity:** the biblical doctrine that the one God subsists in three persons, namely, Father, Son, and Holy Spirit. The word *Trinity* was first used by the Early Church Father Tertullian (ca. 155/160–ca. 220/230) to express what the Scriptures teach about God.

**MAKING CONNECTIONS**

The Invocation—that's how it starts. The common baptismal rite in the Lutheran Church starts with the name of the Father, Son, and Holy Spirit as well. Right from the beginning, we see who is at work here. It's not the person being baptized, the parents of a child, or even the pastor. God is the one working in and through Baptism.

While God does reveal Himself as Father (Exodus 4:22; Isaiah 63:16), Son (2 Samuel 7:13–14; Isaiah 9:6), and Holy Spirit (Psalm 51:11; Isaiah 63:10–11) in the Old Testament, not until the New Testament does God reveal that "Father, Son, and Holy Spirit" is His name and flesh out all that it means that God is a "Tri-unity," or Trinity.

It is in Matthew 28:19 that God's triune name is first given, when Jesus uses the phrase "the name of the Father and of Son and of the Holy Spirit" in connection with Baptism. One thing in particular in our Lord's giving of the triune name is worth unpacking at this point: though there are three parts to God's revealed name, it is still only one name. The Father, the Son, and the Holy Spirit is one God. *Name* is singular. There is a unity and a plurality to God, and Jesus expresses both of these ideas when He reveals to us that Father, Son, and Holy Spirit is *one* name.

## God Gives through His Name

In the Gospel according to John, Jesus says something about God's name that initially strikes us as impossible. He says, "Truly, truly, I say to you, whatever you ask of the Father in My name, He will give it to you" (John 16:23). This sounds pretty extreme. It seems like we can ask for anything and be absolutely sure that we'll receive it. The only qualifier is that we have to ask for it in Jesus' name. A new car. A million dollars in our checking account. A new smart phone with all the latest episodes of *Survivor* loaded onto it. All of these things are ours for the asking. Just end your request with "in Jesus' name," and you'll be sure to get it yesterday.

But that's not what Jesus means. Our Lord isn't giving us a surefire formula to get whatever material thing we want. What Jesus is doing here is telling us that we can always be sure that He will give us all of those things that He gives in His name. Jesus is speaking a lot like He did fifteen hundred years earlier in Numbers 6:27: "So shall they put My name upon the people of Israel, and I will bless them."

In Baptism we receive life, salvation, and the forgiveness of all our sins. These gifts are given in water that is combined with God's Word. They are given in water that is filled with God's name. When we receive the name, we receive the gifts of the name.

This puts a different emphasis on Jesus' words. Whatever we ask the Father in Jesus' name, we will receive, because the promise says that we will always receive what God the Father gives in and with His name. In Baptism, you have the name of God on you. You are a Christian, which means "little Christ." All that God gives to Jesus, He gives to you in Baptism. Every good gift is yours in the moment that the water splashes on your forehead. That is the joy we're going to continue to explore.

We already know some very important things about Baptism. We know that it is a bath that washes away our sin. We know that it puts God's holy name on us. We know that God takes His name seriously and promises to care for any and all who bear it. The next question is, whom is Baptism for—and what does it do for them?

# Study Questions

1. What is the basic meaning of the word used in the Bible for "Baptism"?

2. What does it mean to be born dirty, and what are the consequences?

What can we do about it on our own?

3. Why do we need Baptism to take care of the problem of sin?

4. What part of God's Word is combined with the water of Baptism?

5. By whom was Christian Baptism instituted and when?

Why does it matter that He did this?

6. What is the particular command God gives regarding proper use of His name?

How do we properly use His name, and why is this important?

# Discussion Questions

1. What do you put your name on? What is the significance of your name being there?

2. First-century Jews avoided saying "Yahweh" when they saw it written in the Old Testament. They thought this would guarantee they never misused God's name. Do you think this was a wise way of protecting God's name? Are there ways of misusing it without saying it directly?

   What would be the benefits and drawbacks if modern Christians developed such a practice by not saying "Jesus" or "in the name of the Father and of the Son and of the Holy Spirit"?

3. If, in *The Voyage of the Dawn Treader*, Eustace had been able to get rid of his own dragon skin, what would that have told us about what C. S. Lewis believed about Baptism?

*Visit lutheranism101.com to download the free Leader Guide.*

CHAPTER 2

# A Gift Christ Offers to All People

## In This Chapter

- Christ gives us a mandate to make disciples by baptizing.
- God wants all nations to be baptized, and that means everyone—no exceptions.
- Infants, too, are to be baptized.
- Baptism gives many gifts, including the gift of faith.
- Baptism may come before or after teaching, and there are no prerequisites.

## A Divine Mandate

Baptism is a holy bath in which God washes away all of our sins and puts His name on us. Baptism is able to do these things because God combines water with His own Holy Word and has instituted it for our eternal good and blessing. Because God puts His name on us, He commits Himself to us. He cares for us and protects us from all evil. He even regards us as His children just as He regarded Israel as His child (Exodus 4:22).

When Jesus instituted Baptism, He gave His apostles the mandate to "make disciples of all nations by baptizing them into the name of the Father, the Son, and the Holy Spirit, by teaching them to cherish all things which I have spoken to you" (Matthew 28:19–20, author's translation).

At Jesus' command, people are washed with water that is combined with the name of God. The

**MAKING CONNECTIONS**

The word translated as "cherish" is the New Testament equivalent of the word "keep" in the Aaronic blessing that we looked at in the last chapter. When God puts His name on you, He promises to cherish you. When we are baptized, we are given the joy of cherishing all that Jesus has said!

rest of our Lord's mandate in Matthew 28 and its implications for Baptism hold even more riches.

## Make Disciples

Before Jesus even gets to the word "baptizing," He says that His apostles are to "make disciples." *Disciple* is a difficult word. If you ask three people what it means, you'll probably get four definitions. To understand what Jesus promises about Baptism, we need to mine this word further.

Speaking to a group of Jews who believed in Him, Jesus once said, "If you abide in My word, you are truly My disciples, and you will know the truth, and the truth will set you free" (John 8:31–32). From this passage we know that disciples abide in God's Word. They are like the righteous tree of Psalm 1: "Blessed is the man who walks not in the counsel of the wicked, nor stands in the way of sinners, nor sits in the seat of scoffers; but his delight is in the law of the LORD, and on His law he meditates day and night. He is like a tree planted by streams of water that yields its fruit in its season, and its leaf does not wither. In all that he does, he prospers" (vv. 1–3).

> **FROM THE BIBLE**
>
> For freedom Christ has set us free; stand firm therefore, and do not submit again to a yoke of slavery. (Galatians 5:1)

Disciples know the truth and are freed by it. The psalm we just read puts it this way: "For the LORD knows the way of the righteous, but the way of the wicked will perish" (Psalm 1:6). A disciple is a righteous person, one who has faith in Christ. A disciple trusts Jesus as his or her Savior from sin.

> **FROM THE BIBLE**
>
> For we did not follow cleverly devised myths when we made known to you the power and coming of our Lord Jesus Christ, but we were eyewitnesses of His majesty. (2 Peter 1:16)

### Jesus' Game Plan

Making disciples is what Matthew 28 is all about. Jesus gives the command to make disciples and tells us how this task is accomplished at the same time. This is important. If our Lord had not directly instructed the apostles about how to "make disciples," they would have been left on their own to try to figure it out. They would have had to come up with marketing strategies or brought people in with their sparkling personalities. They would have had to keep trying things until they found something that worked, with no guarantee of success. The good news is that Jesus didn't leave them on their own, and He doesn't leave us to our own devices either. Jesus tells His disciples to make disciples by "baptizing."

This is a word from our Savior. Jesus tells us that through Baptism, a person becomes a disciple, one who trusts Jesus as his or her Savior from sin, death, and the power of the devil. The next question should be fairly obvious: whom is Baptism for?

**MAKING CONNECTIONS**

In the Old Testament, the nations were almost always under God's wrath. Isaiah wrote, "For the LORD is enraged against all the nations, and furious against all their host; He has devoted them to destruction, has given them over for slaughter" (34:2). The mercy that Jesus delivered to them was radical in the extreme.

## All Nations

Baptism is for everybody. Jesus makes this clear when He gives us the gift of Baptism. He says, "Make disciples of all nations." There are no qualifiers. All people everywhere are included in our Lord's command. But as clear as it is, our Lord's inclusion of all people was probably very surprising to the apostles. They were Jews. When Jesus said "all nations," He meant Gentiles (non-Jews) as well as those who were part of the people of Israel. He was talking about people who had never heard of the God of the Bible and those who had. He even meant people in the nations who had been the oppressors of God's people for the past two thousand years. When Jesus said that Baptism was for "all nations," He was saying that it was even for those who had been His enemies.

The Old Testament makes a very consistent distinction between "the nations" (Gentiles) and Israel. Before our Lord came in the flesh, God's people and the Israelites were generally the same group of people. There were certainly examples of Gentiles in the Old Testament who believed in the true God, but for the most part, the people of God in the Old Testament were Israelites or had been incorporated into Israel in some way. In the New Testament, these same people were usually called "Jews." Genetically speaking, the Jews were descended from Abraham, and God had promised eternal blessings to them (Genesis 12:3). In the Old Testament, faithful Israel and the Holy Church were identical. Even though there were certain foreigners who became worshipers of the true God, all of those foreigners were incorporated into the people of Israel in a literal sense—like Rahab, Ruth, and Bathsheba—or in a spiritual way—like the people of Nineveh who believed when Jonah prophesied to them (Jonah 3:5).

## Expanding the Borders

In the Old Testament, the nations were filled with idolatrous, pagan peoples who worshiped false gods. The Scriptures frequently contrast these false gods with the true God, the God of Israel. "Are there any among the false gods of the nations that can bring rain? Or can the heavens give showers? Are you not He, O LORD our God? We set our hope on You, for You do all these things" (Jeremiah 14:22).

In our Lord's command to baptize all nations, the boundaries of the true, spiritual Israel are expanded. After Jesus institutes Baptism, becoming part of the nation-state of Israel is no longer the ordinary way in which a person becomes a worshiper of the true God. Jesus does something new. His Gospel—the Baptism that He institutes—is for all people everywhere. This includes all nations: Israel *and* the rest of them.

In Baptism, Jesus fulfills the prophecy that He spoke to Abraham: "In you all the families of the earth shall be blessed" (Genesis 12:3). Baptism is the means that Jesus establishes in the New Testament to deliver the blessing. "All nations" in Baptism and "all the families of the earth" in God's promise to Abraham refer to exactly the same people.

**MAKING CONNECTIONS**

Other than Mary and Tamar, the only women who are mentioned in Jesus' genealogy in Matthew 1:1–17 are foreigners who had become Israelites: Rahab, Ruth, and Bathsheba.

**FROM THE BIBLE**

For all have sinned and fall short of the glory of God, and are justified by His grace as a gift, through the redemption that is in Christ Jesus. (Romans 3:23–24)

## Questioning "All Nations"

Many Christians raise a question about our Lord's command. What is the extent of "all nations"? Does it really mean every man, woman, child, and infant in every nation? Instead, are there qualifications that make this group a bit smaller, a bit more specific—limiting factors that we just don't see when we read Matthew 28:19–20 on its own?

There are several Bible passages that clarify just what Jesus means by "all nations." He really does mean "everyone."

## What Shall We Do?

Shortly after Jesus commanded His apostles to make disciples of all nations, the time came for the Feast of Pentecost, or the Feast of Weeks. Celebrated each year fifty days after the Passover, Pentecost was one of the festivals for which the Jewish faithful were required to travel to Jerusalem. This means that there were observant Jews from all over the Roman world. In his account of the day, Luke lists many of the places that the pilgrims had come from: Parthia, Media, Elam, Mesopotamia, Judea, Cappadocia, Pontus, Asia, Phrygia, Pamphylia, Egypt, Libya, Rome, Crete, and Arabia (Acts 2:9–11).

**FROM THE BIBLE**

And they were amazed and astonished, saying, "Are not all these who are speaking Galileans? And how is it that we hear, each of us in his own native language?" (Acts 2:7–8)

**FROM THE BIBLE**

Men of Israel, hear these words: Jesus of Nazareth, a man attested to you by God with mighty works and wonders and signs that God did through Him in your midst, as you yourselves know—this Jesus, delivered up according to the definite plan and foreknowledge of God, you crucified and killed by the hands of lawless men. God raised Him up, loosing the pangs of death, because it was not possible for Him to be held by it. (Acts 2:22–24)

As this diverse crowd gathered to celebrate the festival, Peter and the other apostles gathered together to preach the Gospel. To make sure that everyone there heard the Gospel clearly, the Holy Spirit descended on the apostles and gave them the ability to preach in all of the languages of those present.

Then Peter preached a sermon about what had happened at the Passover fifty days before. It was then that Jesus had been arrested by the Jewish leaders in Jerusalem, handed over to the Roman authorities, flogged, crucified, and raised from the dead. Many of those gathered probably didn't know until that moment what had happened at the Passover. They were hearing about who Jesus actually was for the first time.

After the sermon was over, several who heard it were cut to the heart and asked Peter, "What shall we do?" (Acts 2:37). Peter's response gives us a helpful explanation of what Jesus means by "all nations" in Matthew 28:19. Peter said, "Repent and be baptized every one of you in the name of Jesus Christ for the forgiveness of your sins, and you will receive the gift of the Holy Spirit. For the promise is for you and for your children and for all who are far off, everyone whom the Lord our God calls to Himself" (Acts 2:38–39).

## For You and Your Children

Notice who Peter says Baptism is for. First, he says it is for "every one of you," but he doesn't stop there. He goes on to say that the promise is for "you and for your children and for all who are far off." Peter is very clear. The gift of Baptism and the forgiveness of sins that God promises to give through it are for all people. Baptism is for all who heard and believed on that day, all who are in their families, and even all those who are far off and know nothing of the salvation that Christ has won for them. Baptism is for each and every one of them.

After Peter encouraged his hearers to be baptized, they took him at his word. Luke wrote, "So those who received his word were baptized, and there were added that day about three thousand souls" (Acts 2:41). Pentecost was not, however, an isolated incident. Later in the Book of Acts, Paul and Silas baptized the entire family of a jailer at Philippi (Acts 16:25–34). All in the family were baptized. There was no discrimination on the basis of age, gender, nationality, or anything else. The Philippian jailer and his family were definitely part of the "all nations" that Jesus had been talking about when He instituted Baptism.

## Baptism and Faith

As clear as it is from passages like Matthew 28, Acts 2, and Acts 16 that Baptism is a gift that Christ offers to all people, for some these passages are not enough. They argue that a person can only be baptized if he or she confesses the faith and asks for it. They say that in order to have true faith in Christ, a person has to decide to believe. They also say that only someone who already has faith in Christ should be baptized.

If these assertions were true, there would be several classes of people who would be completely excluded from the baptismal life. We would never be able to baptize infants, small children, those with certain cognitive challenges, or even the extremely aged. Some

**TECHNICAL STUFF**

All of the Lord's Means of Grace (Baptism, Absolution, the Lord's Supper, and God's Word) are universal in their scope. They are gifts that God intends everyone to enjoy. The primary reason is a simple one: the Means of Grace deliver in time what Jesus won for all people on the cross. Because Jesus' death is for everyone, the Means of Grace are too.

**FROM THE BIBLE**

For this is the covenant that I will make with the house of Israel after those days, declares the LORD: I will put My law within them, and I will write it on their hearts. And I will be their God, and they shall be My people. And no longer shall each one teach his neighbor and each his brother, saying, "Know the LORD," for they shall all know Me, ***from the least of them to the greatest***, declares the LORD. For I will forgive their iniquity, and I will remember their sin no more. (Jeremiah 31:33–34, emphasis added)

**NEED TO KNOW**

**Disciple:** In the ancient world, a disciple was a person who learned all that his master taught and put it into practice. In the Scriptures, one becomes a disciple through Baptism. It is entirely a gift of God. Baptized Christians will delight in the study of God's Word. Note that while they will study God's Word because they are disciples, they are not disciples simply because they study God's Word.

**NEED TO KNOW**

**Divine Passive:** a place in the Scriptures where the One performing an action is not named but is understood to be God Himself. When Peter encourages Baptism in Acts 2:38, he says "be baptized," but he never says who does the Baptism. The reason is simple. God baptizes. One of the best ways to rightly confess Baptism is to remember that God is the one acting and we are the ones receiving.

of these people would never be able to receive the gift of Baptism, because they would never be able to make a conscious decision to believe, and they would never be able to ask for Baptism either. The good news for us is that as popular as these approaches are, they cannot bear much scrutiny. Each position makes fundamental mistakes about what Baptism is and does.

## Is Faith in Christ an Absolute Requirement for Baptism?

It is already clear from the Lord's words that faith in Christ cannot be a requirement for Baptism. Whenever a person says faith is necessary prior to Baptism, he or she does so by ignoring, denying, or redefining one or more of the things Jesus said when He instituted Baptism in Matthew 28:19.

The specific part of our Lord's command that is misunderstood by making faith a precondition for Baptism is "make disciples." We have seen that a disciple is one who has faith in Christ. A disciple is one who knows the truth and has been set free by it. One could actually say that being a disciple of Christ and having faith in Christ mean the same thing. It wouldn't make any sense to say that someone has to be a disciple in order to be made into a disciple. It would be a little like saying that milk has to be cheese in order to become cheese. But that's not the way it works. Not all milk is cheese even though all cheese comes from milk.

Those who misunderstand Baptism in this way will argue that being a disciple is much more than having faith in Christ. They will say that a disciple is a believer in Christ who has made a special commitment to Him and that Baptism is the first step in this process of commitment. As common as this idea is, it won't be found in the Bible. In Scripture, a disciple is one who has been set free by knowing the truth. In Scripture, the only way to know the truth is to have received the forgiveness of sins in the first place (Luke 1:77). Finally, in Scripture, Baptism is one way in which we see that there are no spiritual distinctions or ranks among Christians. "For as many of you as were baptized into Christ have put on Christ. There is neither Jew nor Greek, there is neither slave nor free, there is no male and female, for you are all one in Christ Jesus" (Galatians 3:27–28).

**MAKING CONNECTIONS**

In Romans 3, Paul teaches us that just as all people have sinned, all people are justified through Jesus' atoning work on the cross. Since Baptism delivers the forgiveness that Jesus won for us, it is absolutely necessary that it be a gift for all the people for whom Jesus died, whether they are young or old, mentally alert or suffering from dementia.

## No Exceptions

The part of our Lord's command that is misunderstood by those who make faith a requirement for Baptism is "all nations." "All nations" doesn't exclude anyone. Even though the phrase itself would be enough for us to know this, we have many other good reasons to think this way. Both in Acts 2 and 16, the Bible makes it clear that "all nations" means "all people" and that there are no distinctions made among people on the basis of age or mental ability.

If the Scriptures weren't enough—though they certainly are—we also have the whole history of the Christian Church. From even the second century, there is evidence that the Church has always baptized babies. When Polycarp, the bishop of Smyrna, was martyred for the faith, he said that he had been serving Jesus for eighty-six years. Since that was Polycarp's age, he was hinting that he had been baptized as a baby.

## Letting God Do the Work

Luther also explains how Baptism is for everyone. Wisely, he points us back to the Lord's command and promise. He argues that if we say that Baptism depends upon our faith, we no longer confess that Baptism is God's work for us, and we make it into our work for God instead.

"We are not very concerned to know whether the person baptized believes or not. For Baptism does not become invalid on that account. But everything depends on God's Word and command. . . . That is, when the Word is added to the water, Baptism is valid, even though faith is lacking. For my faith does not make Baptism, but receives it. Now, Baptism does not become invalid even though it is wrongly received or used. As stated above, it is not bound to our faith, but to the Word" (LC IV 52–53).

## Is It Necessary for One Being Baptized to Make a Conscious Decision?

Another way in which some try to exclude the very young from the gift of Baptism is to say that one who is very young—a baby, for example—is not able to ask for Baptism. Those who think of Baptism in this way will say that if a person doesn't ask for it, it's not a real Baptism. This, however, is an error very similar to the one just addressed.

Someone who takes this approach to Baptism believes that the person being baptized is the one actually at work in the Baptism. In this scenario, the person being baptized takes place number one and God takes place number two. The person's act of will—saying that he or she wants to be baptized—becomes the most important element in the entire Baptism. Our Lord's mandate and Word aren't mentioned. Water doesn't even get honorable mention. Baptism is, in this case, entirely the act of a person's will.

In order to make Baptism something that the person being baptized does, one has to ignore the Lord's mandate completely. There are exactly zero places where God describes Baptism in Scripture as something that the person being baptized does. Just as we do not ask to be born, we do not need to request to be reborn in Baptism. There are no prerequisites, no mental or emotional milestones we have to achieve first. It doesn't require faith or holiness on our part. The faith and holiness are provided by the One doing the baptizing, by God Himself, which is why He is the only one who can take center stage in the action of Baptism.

**FROM THE BIBLE**

The natural person does not accept the things of the Spirit of God, for they are folly to him, and he is not able to understand them because they are spiritually discerned. (1 Corinthians 2:14)

**MAKING CONNECTIONS**

In John 6:44, Jesus says, "No one can come to Me unless the Father who sent Me draws him. And I will raise him up on the last day." Whenever a person comes to faith in Christ through Baptism or through hearing the Lord's Word, it is God the Father who is acting through His Holy Spirit.

## Let the Little Children Come to Me

The Gospel of Luke records an event that has several important things to say about whether babies should be baptized. People were bringing infants to Jesus so that He could touch them, but the disciples tried to send them away. To the disciples, blessing babies was not a good use of Jesus' time.

What our Lord said in reply is very important. He said, "Let the children come to Me, and do not hinder them, for to such belongs the kingdom of God. Truly, I say to you, whoever does not receive the kingdom of God like a child shall not enter it" (Luke 18:16–17).

In verse 15, the word that Luke used to describe the children was "infants." The Greek term refers to babies who are still nursing at their mothers' breasts. It was about this sort of child that Jesus said "do not hinder them" and "to such belongs the kingdom of God."

## The Extraordinary "Ordinary Means"

It is precisely in Baptism that one receives the kingdom of God. Just as infants are entirely dependent upon others for everything they need, those who receive the kingdom of God do so not by their own efforts but entirely as a gift. Jesus has given us Baptism as the normal means by which we enter God's kingdom.

Since Baptism is the ordinary means by which we enter the kingdom of God, it is perfectly legitimate for us to read Luke 18 in light of the gift of Baptism. In Luke 18, Jesus is teaching us whom the kingdom of God is for and how we enter it. Considering all that we've already read in Matthew and Acts, it's difficult to imagine a reading of this passage that doesn't involve Baptism. This passage also shows us that infants can and do have faith.

## Bouncing Baby Baptist

Luke establishes the ability of infants to have faith very early in His Gospel. John the Baptist leaps for joy in his mother's womb when Jesus comes near (Luke 1:41). Luke's Gospel also begins with two conceptions. The first is John the Baptist's. John is born to Zechariah, a temple priest, and his wife, Elizabeth. John is conceived when both of his parents are extremely old.

Even before he is born, John is filled with the Holy Spirit (Luke 1:15). When Elizabeth is sixth months pregnant with John, Mary, who is already pregnant with Jesus, comes to Jerusalem to visit her cousin Elizabeth. As soon as Mary meets Elizabeth, John leaps in his mother's womb. Tiny John the Baptist's joy is over having a Savior and being in His presence. This is reminiscent of a statement in the Psalms: "Upon You I have leaned from before my birth; You are He who took me from my mother's womb. My praise is continually of You" (Psalm 71:6).

## Babies in Need

There's a final, critical point about our Lord's desire to include little babies in the gift of Baptism: Jesus welcomes babies into His kingdom because they need what Baptism offers. Romans 3:10–11 says, "None is righteous, no, not one; no one understands; no one seeks for God." Passages like Psalm 51:5 prove that babies are not an exception. Babies are sinners just as we all are.

Babies need the salvation that Christ won for them on the cross. Babies need forgiveness. The clearest evidence of this is also devastatingly tragic. Babies die. It happens thousands of times each year just in the United States, and God's Word is clear about where death comes from: "The wages of sin is death" (Romans 6:23). We are all born as slaves to sin, but unlike some slave owners, our master pays a sure and certain wage: death. We die because we sin, and we sin even before we are born.

If we deny babies the gift of Baptism, we are denying them what Jesus wants to give to them. We are *not* letting the little children come to Him, and we *are* hindering them. This we must not do. Jesus has words about that as well. When He talks about any who would tempt a "little one" , Jesus says, "It would be better for him if a millstone were hung around his neck and he were cast into the sea than that he should cause one of these little ones to sin" (Luke 17:2).

## Cut into the Covenant

One last way to see whom Baptism is for is by looking at the corresponding rite in the Old Testament: circumcision. Paul makes the point that Baptism replaces circumcision in his Letter to the Colossians. "In Him also you were circumcised with a circumcision made without hands, by putting off the body of the flesh, by the circumcision of Christ, having been buried with Him in baptism, in which you were also raised with Him through faith in the powerful working of God, who raised Him from the dead" (Colossians 2:11–12).

In the Old Testament, God instituted circumcision to be a physical sign that a person was part of God's covenant people. Circumcision was, for obvious reasons, irrevocable. Once a boy was circumcised, he was circumcised forever. Though an Israelite might abandon the faith into which he had been circumcised and begin to worship the false gods of the surrounding nations, his circumcision would remain. Until he died, he would still be marked as one who belonged to the Lord and bore His name.

**NEED TO KNOW**

**Circumcision:** the surgical removal of the foreskin from a boy's penis. For the Israelites, though the males were the ones marked physically by circumcision, it was a sign for the women as well. Through their fathers and husbands and sons, women were partners in the covenant promises.

## The Eighth Day

According to the law that guided them, every male Israelite was circumcised on the eighth day (Leviticus 12:3), and he would formally become a part of the covenant people.

It goes without saying that eight days is extremely young. It is the first day of the second week of a child's life. If Baptism corresponds to circumcision, then Baptism is also for the extremely young.

The eighth day has become one of the Church's most beloved symbols of what God does in Baptism. God created the entire universe in six days. He rested on the seventh. This was the basis upon which God established the regular workweek in the Old Testament. His people were to work for six days and rest on the seventh. Though we can know from astronomy that there are 365 days in a year, the seven-day week is something we only know through divine revelation.

The eighth day of a week is, of course, the first day of the following week. Because of this, the number eight has become associated in the Church with renewal and rebirth. In a similar way, seven is the number of completeness and perfection because it is the number of days in a week, and six is the number of imperfection and the world because it is one less than seven.

## Eight Sides to Every Story

In the Ancient Church, there were sometimes special buildings called "baptisteries" in which all Baptisms took place. These buildings almost always had eight sides. In the modern Church, the symbol continues with the many baptismal fonts that have eight sides in order to confess the new life that we have in Baptism.

My favorite example of this is the baptismal font at the Chapel of Saint Timothy and Saint Titus at Concordia Seminary in St. Louis. At the top of the font, you will see the traditional eight sides that you see in many fonts. But that's not where the confession of Baptism ends. The base of the font has six sides, and the column between the top and bottom consists of three circular poles. That particular font confesses that in Baptism, you go from sin and imperfection to new life through the name of the holy and blessed Trinity.

**MAKING CONNECTIONS**

Another connection for eight-sided baptismal fonts is the story of Noah. Eight people were brought to new life through the waters that destroyed sinful humankind. We, too, are carried in an ark, the ark of the Church. This in turn can be seen in the design of many older church sanctuaries, constructed to look like upside-down boats.

## Baptizing/Teaching

At the same time our Lord institutes Baptism, He also commissions His disciples to make disciples "by teaching them to cherish all things which [He has] spoken to [them]" (Matthew 28:20, author's translation). When Jesus says this, He connects the command to baptize to the command to teach. There is nothing separating the two phrases. In English, we would normally use a word like *and* to connect them, but Jesus doesn't do this. The activities of baptizing and teaching are so closely related that Jesus doesn't even separate them from each other with a little two- or three-letter word.

**MAKING CONNECTIONS**

We have examples in Scripture of teaching before Baptism (the Ethiopian eunuch) as well as of Baptism before teaching (Peter's sermon at Pentecost). We would have to ignore these and other biblical examples in order to use only one of these approaches.

### The Chicken and the Egg

The proximity of the phrases "baptizing" and "teaching" in our Lord's command have often led Christians to have a "chicken and the egg" argument about the practice of Baptism. The question is this: should one be taught before being baptized, or should one be baptized before being taught?

The answer is simple: yes. While there are times when Baptism will necessarily precede teaching, there are also circumstances in which teaching will normally come before Baptism. The most important point that Jesus makes by having "baptizing" and "teaching" side by side in the mandate is that the two should, in one way or another, always come together.

### Baptism as Conversion

When Christian parents receive the gift of a new child, the normal practice in the Church is for those parents to bring that child to church to receive the gift of Baptism. You can guess the reasons for this. The parents know from the Scriptures that their child is a sinner in need of forgiveness. They know that their child is one for whom God has established and given Baptism. They know that in Baptism their child will receive the forgiveness of sins and become a disciple of Christ.

Some parents feel such an urgency that they ask their pastor to meet them in the hospital when the child is born. They want their child to receive the gift of Baptism as quickly as possible. Some wait a little longer. Whatever the particular practice might be in the case of a particular child, Christian parents who know what Baptism is and what God gives through it are always going to want their child to receive that gift soon after birth.

When we say that in Baptism the child receives the forgiveness of sins, life, and salvation, we are saying that in Baptism the child is converted. Many Christians think it is very important to have a "conversion experience." They want a person to be able to give a date and even a time for the moment that he or she became a Christian. Sadly, most of these Christians do not acknowledge that for one who is baptized as a baby, the conversion to the Christian faith happened in the moment that the name of the triune God was poured on that person with the baptismal waters.

## A Glorious Moment

Ironically, Christians who were baptized when they were babies can give an absolutely sure and certain date and time that they became Christians. Some of them may even have photographs of the moment. I once attended a church that confessed this reality in a beautiful way. Whenever a person was baptized, the congregation would immediately respond by singing, "Alleluia! Alleluia! Alleluia!" as soon as the words "I baptize you in the name of the Father and of the Son and of the Holy Spirit" were spoken. The congregation could not restrain its joy. It had to respond to the miracle of faith that God had given by singing praises to Him.

## Listen Up, Babies!

In the case of infant Baptism, it is impossible for teaching to precede Baptism. A baby who is just a few minutes, days, or weeks old cannot understand human language. If we were to require children to be instructed in the Christian faith before receiving the gift of Baptism, they would not receive those gifts until several years after their birth.

**MAKING CONNECTIONS**

In the parable of the lost sheep, Jesus says that "there is joy before the angels of God over one sinner who repents" (Luke 15:10). When a person is baptized into Christ, he or she receives faith in Christ and, through that faith, turns aside (repents) from all sins. This means that there is rejoicing in the presence of the angels. Who is rejoicing? God!

**MAKING CONNECTIONS**

After Baptism, the pastor says, "In Holy Baptism God the Father has made you a member of His Son, our Lord Jesus Christ, and an heir with us of all the treasures of heaven in the one holy Christian and apostolic Church. We receive you in Jesus' name as our ***brother/sister*** in Christ, that together we might hear His Word, receive His gifts, and proclaim the praises of Him who called us out of darkness into His marvelous light." The congregation responds, "Amen. We welcome you in the name of the Lord" (*LSB*, p. 271).

Of course, infant Baptism certainly doesn't keep someone from receiving instruction in the Christian faith. The instruction actually does not need to be delayed at all. Paul gives us a promise in Romans 10:17: "So faith comes from hearing, and hearing through the word of Christ." Faith comes from hearing, not from understanding. If we really had to *understand* the Word of God in order to receive benefits from it, none of us would ever get anything from Scripture. But the promise of God does not depend on us in any way. When we hear the Word of God, He blesses us through it.

Romans 10 isn't the only place where Paul makes this point. He says this rather directly in a letter that he writes to a young pastor named Timothy. He says, "From infancy you have known the Holy Scriptures" (2 Timothy 3:15, author's translation). The word that Paul uses in this verse for an infant is the same one that Luke uses in Luke 18:15 when people are bringing their children to Jesus to have Him bless them. Infants, even nursing babes, can know the Holy Scriptures. How can this be? The most likely answer is that Timothy's mother and grandmother brought Timothy to the waters of Baptism as a baby and then made sure that he was present in the worship services of the Church, where then, even as a baby, he heard the Word of God read and preached (2 Timothy 1:5).

**FROM THE BIBLE**

I am reminded of your sincere faith, a faith that dwelt first in your grandmother Lois and your mother Eunice and now, I am sure, dwells in you as well. (2 Timothy 1:5)

## In the Parish to Cherish

The instruction of a baptized baby begins when he or she is brought into the worship life of the Church. There is no child too young to benefit from hearing God's Word read and proclaimed. That is the beginning of a child being taught to "cherish all things which I have spoken to you" (Matthew 28:20, author's translation).

**TECHNICAL STUFF**

Many translations shy away from the word "infancy" in 2 Timothy 3:15, making the connection to Luke 18 unclear.

As a child grows in years, his or her parents and sponsors are to "pray for them" and "support them in their ongoing instruction and nurture in the Christian faith" (*LSB*, p. 269). In the Lutheran tradition, this often culminates in two or three years of intensive instruction in the Christian faith that precedes their first reception of the Lord's Supper. This, however, is a bit different from what our Lord is talking about in Matthew 28.

Teaching a baptized Christian to "cherish all things which [Jesus has] spoken to you" is a lifelong activity. The baptized Christian never outgrows study of God's Word and instruction in the Christian faith. The Christian always desires to learn more of how God has revealed Himself in the Scriptures precisely *because* he or she is baptized and this is what the baptized always want to do.

**MAKING CONNECTIONS**

Instruction in the faith and study of God's Word should be part of the daily routine for any Christian. When Moses instructed Israel in the way they should study God's Word, this is what he said: "And these words that I command you today shall be on your heart. You shall teach them diligently to your children, and shall talk of them when you sit in your house, and when you walk by the way, and when you lie down, and when you rise. You shall bind them as a sign on your hand, and they shall be as frontlets between your eyes. You shall write them on the doorposts of your house and on your gates" (Deuteronomy 6:6–9).

## Baptism Following Conversion

We've already heard the story of the Ethiopian eunuch. In this story, Philip is sent by the Holy Spirit to speak to an Ethiopian court official as he travels home from visiting Jerusalem. He is reading from the scroll of Isaiah. "Like a sheep He was led to the slaughter and like a lamb before its shearer is silent, so He opens not His mouth. In His humiliation justice was denied Him. Who can describe His generation? For His life is taken away from the earth" (Acts 8:32–33).

Philip asks the eunuch if he understands what he's reading, and the eunuch says that he can't unless someone explains it to him. Luke continues his telling of the story by saying this: "Then Philip opened his mouth, and beginning with this Scripture he told him the good news about Jesus" (Acts 8:35).

You already know what happens next. They pass by some water and the eunuch says, "See, here is water! What prevents me from being baptized?" (Acts 8:36). The question is, when Philip explained the Scriptures to the eunuch, what did he say? From Luke's description and the eunuch's response, we can conclude several things. First, we know that Philip told the eunuch that Jesus was the fulfillment of the Old Testament prophecy that the eunuch had been reading. Second, we know that Philip taught the eunuch about the gifts that God offers in Baptism.

We know this because of the eunuch's response. After being taught by Philip, the eunuch wanted nothing more than to receive the gifts God offers in Baptism. He heard the Word of God, responded to it in faith, and requested the gift through which Christ would decisively bring him into the kingdom of God.

**BELIEVE, TEACH, CONFESS**

In the Preface to his Small Catechism, Luther writes, "Therefore dear brothers, for God's sake I beg all of you who are pastors and preachers to devote yourselves sincerely to the duties of your office, that you feel compassion for the people entrusted to your care, and that you help us accordingly to inculcate this catechism in the people, especially the young" (Preface, 6).

It is because of the example of the Ethiopian eunuch that it has always been the most common practice among Christians to instruct adults in the Christian faith before receiving them into the Church through Baptism. When adults become Christians, God gives them the gift of faith through the proclamation of the Word. Listening to the Word of God, these Christians—like the assembled Jews on Pentecost—are cut to the heart and believe the Gospel.

## I Have to Wait How Long?

The amount of instruction that an adult catechumen (learner) receives can vary. In the Church of St. Augustine in the fourth century, catechumens were instructed for three years before being baptized on the Vigil of Easter. During Lent, these catechumens were immersed in an intensive seven weeks of instruction, which culminated in learning the Apostles' Creed and the Lord's Prayer. Many Lutheran churches instruct adults using *Luther's Small Catechism with Explanation* before baptizing them into the Christian faith.

Pastors often have to make judgment calls about when it makes the most sense to baptize a person. Sometimes, as in the case of the Ethiopian eunuch, a pastor may baptize a Christian because that person has heard what God offers in Baptism, desires to receive it, and asks for it with great urgency. Sometimes a pastor may want to wait until the catechumen more fully understands the articles of the Christian faith before receiving him or her into the Church through Baptism.

Whatever the circumstances, we know one thing with absolute certainty: Baptism is a gift through which Christ gives the forgiveness of sins, and He has offered this gift to all people of all ages and all levels of mental capacity. He desires all to be baptized into Him. This reality leads us to an extended discussion of an important question that we've only given the broad strokes on so far: what does Baptism do?

# Study Questions

1. What does Jesus mean by the phrase "all nations"?

2. What does the phrase "make disciples" in Matthew 28 teach us about what Baptism does?

3. Why is the eighth day a symbol of renewal and rebirth, and how is this reflected in many churches' baptismal practices?

4. What special confidence do Christians who have their children baptized as infants possess, and conversely, what do those who wait miss out on?

*Visit lutheranism101.com to download the free Leader Guide.*

5. In Lutheranism, when is Baptism ordinarily received before instruction in the Christian faith, and when does instruction normally come first? In each case, why?

# Discussion Questions

1. The Scriptures never talk about "adults of God." How do Jesus' words about "little children" apply to all of us?

2. Christ commands us to go to "all nations," baptizing and teaching. What are the implications of this for mission work?

   How about domestically and within our own churches?

3. How would our theology of Baptism be different if when the Ethiopian eunuch saw the water, he had said, "There is water! I could be baptized, but that's not really necessary since I already believe that Jesus is my Savior"?

*Visit lutheranism101.com to download the free Leader Guide.*

PUTTING IT ALL TOGETHER

# A Word for Our Sponsors

Referred to elsewhere as "godparents," sponsors are an incredibly important part of providing a spiritual support network for the person being baptized.

Here's what is said about sponsors in the Lutheran baptismal rite:

> From ancient times the Church has observed the custom of appointing sponsors for baptismal candidates and catechumens. In the Evangelical Lutheran Church sponsors are to confess the faith expressed in the Apostles' Creed and taught in the Small Catechism. They are, whenever possible, to witness the Baptism of those they sponsor. They are to pray for them, support them in their ongoing instruction and nurture in the Christian faith, and encourage them toward the faithful reception of the Lord's Supper. They are at all times to be examples to them of the holy life of faith in Christ and love for the neighbor. (*LSB*, p. 269)

Following this, the pastor asks for their willingness to serve as sponsors and blesses them: "God enable you both to will and to do this faithful and loving work and with His grace fulfill what we are unable to do" (p. 269).

Sponsors are long-term supporters and teachers of the person sponsored. It is a blessed position with responsibilities that must be taken seriously.

The book *The Baptism of Your Child* expands on this further:

> In Baptism, your child will be made a part of a new family—

> the Holy Christian Church. This means the members of the Church are now your child's siblings. Because your child's brothers and sisters have an interest in their new sibling, sponsors are usually assigned to your child. These sponsors are representatives of the Church and are asked to support and encourage the parents in the ongoing nurture of the baptized child. If necessary, the sponsors act as parental substitutes attending to the faith of the baptized, should the child lose his or her parents. For this reason, the selection of sponsors should be made with care. It is most fitting for the sponsors to be selected from among the faithful of the congregation. At the least, the sponsors should believe and confess the faith into which the child is being baptized. (Fast and Fast, p. 23)

Sponsors—yet one more blessing we receive at the time of our Baptism!

# PART TWO

## What you'll learn about:

- Through Baptism, we are brought into the Father's royal family, with the Church as our Mother, and Christ as our Brother.
- Baptism makes us heirs of all God's gifts, including forgiveness of sins, eternal life, and salvation.
- As a priesthood of believers, we are to proudly bear God's name.
- From conception, we are dead in our sins and cannot save ourselves.
- We are baptized into Christ's death and resurrection and are cleansed by His blood.
- Contrary to appearances, God is the one who is active in Baptism, not us.

# What Does Baptism Do?

Perhaps a better question would be "What *Doesn't* Baptism Do?" It makes us God's royal heirs, forgives our sins, and connects us to Christ. But that's not all. Baptism is the ultimate birth, the ultimate bath, and the ultimate portal to eternal life. In short, Baptism does the very things we need it to do the most.

CHAPTER 3

# Birth into the Royal Family

## In This Chapter

- Baptism is both new birth and adoption into God's royal family.
- God is our loving Father, the Church our Mother, and Christ our Brother.
- We are heirs of forgiveness and God's own unending life.

**MAKING CONNECTIONS**

God's own child, I gladly say it:
I am baptized into Christ!
He, because I could not pay it,
Gave my full redemption price.
Do I need earth's treasures many?
I have one worth more than any
That brought me salvation free
Lasting to eternity! (*LSB* 594:1)

## A Royal Family

The birth of a baby is a time of excitement for the whole family. As the days go on, the new parents become more and more aware that their lives have changed forever. Their entire focus changes. The family is not just husband and wife anymore. Now it's husband, wife, and baby. The parents begin to think about everything in terms of what's best for the child. How are we going to raise the child? How can we make the house more safe? How can we eat healthier so that our child grows up enjoying the best sorts of food? How are we going to educate the baby? Where are we going to find the money to provide for all of the baby's needs?

When a child is born into a royal family, the stakes are even higher in some ways. When Prince William of England married Catherine Middleton in April 2011, everyone knew that they were probably seeing the mother of a future monarch. But Catherine was a commoner. The blood of queens did not flow through her veins. When she was born, her parents did not expect that she could eventually be the mother of a king or queen. All of that changed when Catherine married the man who was second in the line of succession to the British throne. And when their hopes to expand their family became public, the media went wild with speculation that a baby would soon be born into the royal family.

Baptism should give us even greater excitement than England feels at the prospect of a future king or queen being born. The crown of a human monarch is temporary and fleeting. Eventually, Elizabeth II and all of her descendants will be dead and buried, just like all of her ancestors. Their crowns will crumble into dust, but Baptism is different. In Baptism, a person is born into God's royal family and receives a crown that will last for all eternity. This is why King Louis IX of France (St. Louis) always signed official documents with the name "Louis of Poissy." Poissy is where Louis was baptized. Louis treasured the place of his Baptism far above the cathedral in which he was crowned the king of France. For all of their earthly magnificence, that cathedral and that crown were not important to him at all.

## Born from Below and from Above

### From Below

Early in our Lord's ministry, a member of the ruling council of the Jews in Jerusalem named Nicodemus came to Jesus under the cover of darkness. Nicodemus had heard about Jesus and wanted to learn from Him, but he didn't want his colleagues in the Sanhedrin to know that he was interested in what Jesus was teaching.

In His conversation with Nicodemus, Jesus focused the discussion on what distinguishes physical birth from spiritual birth. Initially His words were very confusing to Nicodemus. Jesus said, "Unless one is born again he cannot see the kingdom of God" (John 3:3). The word translated as "again" has two possible meanings. The word is usually translated as "again" because it is clear that Nicodemus understood it that way. He replied, "How can a man be born when he is old? Can he enter *a second time* into his mother's womb and be born?" (John 3:4, emphasis added). By saying "a second time," Nicodemus reveals that he thinks Jesus is talking about a second birth. He thinks the word means "again."

Nicodemus is technically right, but he is right in an incomplete way. He doesn't really understand what Jesus is saying. Even though Jesus has not yet instituted Baptism at the time He has this

**NEED TO KNOW**

**Sanhedrin:** the ruling council of the Jews in Jerusalem that was led by the high priest during the period after the Babylonian exile (seventh century BC). The Sanhedrin handed Jesus over to Pontius Pilate to be crucified. At least two members of the Sanhedrin (Nicodemus and Joseph of Arimathea) probably objected because they believed that Jesus was the Messiah.

conversation, it is clear from context and from the way that John writes his Gospel that Baptism is what Jesus is referring to here. John was writing to baptized Christians who were probably already familiar with the Gospels of Matthew, Mark, and Luke. Because of the imagery that John uses here, it would have been obvious to any of his readers that Jesus was talking to Nicodemus about Baptism. The Bible often talks about Baptism in the way Jesus is speaking in this passage. Baptism is both new birth and adoption into God's family. In Titus 3:5 (NIV), Baptism is called a "washing of rebirth and renewal by the Holy Spirit."

**MAKING CONNECTIONS**

It is also in Jesus' conversation with Nicodemus about Baptism that He speaks some of His most beautiful words: "For God so loved the world, that He gave His only Son, that whoever believes in Him should not perish but have eternal life" (John 3:16).

## From Above

The second meaning of the word that is translated as "again" is "from above." Two verses later, Jesus makes it clear that He is also using the word in that way. He says, "Unless one is born of water and the Spirit, he cannot enter the kingdom of God. That which is born of the flesh is flesh, and that which is born of the Spirit is spirit" (John 3:5–6). Jesus is saying that Christians have a first birth that is physical and fleshly (from below) and are then born again from above. When Nicodemus thought Jesus was talking about a second birth, he was right, but he didn't know the kind of birth that Jesus was referring to.

It is impossible to overstate the significance of our Lord's words to Nicodemus. We all know something about the joy that human parents have in the birth of their own children. Even if you're not a parent, you've seen the light in the eyes of new parents. If you have children, then you know the joy all the more clearly. It is not a stretch at all to say that God experiences similar joy whenever a sinner is baptized. This is quite possibly in the background of what Jesus says at the end of the parable of the lost coin: "Just so, I tell you, there is joy before the angels of God over one sinner who repents" (Luke 15:10). In Baptism, we receive faith in Christ. In Baptism, our sins are washed away. In Baptism, we turn away (repent) from the life our sinful flesh wants to live. When this happens, there is joy before the angels of God. But who is rejoicing before the angels of God? It should be obvious by now. It's the proud Papa.

## Who's Your Daddy?

Nicodemus was confused by what Jesus said about Baptism, because he thought about birth in purely physical terms. He knew that at some point in the past, his mother had been pregnant and had then given birth to him. He may have even had children of his own and seen their births with his own eyes. He knew what it was to be born. He knew that birth was a one-time event, and it had already happened for him many years before.

**FROM THE BIBLE**

Israel is My firstborn son. (Exodus 4:22)

On the face of it, Nicodemus's confusion makes a lot more sense to us than our Lord's response does. We have one father, one mother, and we were born one time. It's simple biology. But Jesus talks about two fathers, two mothers, and two births. Understanding what He's getting at requires carefully reading what the Bible has to say about how God is our Father.

### Abba! Father!

In his sermon at Pentecost, Peter promised that all who are baptized "receive the gift of the Holy Spirit" (Acts 2:38). In his Letter to the Romans, Paul tells us what the Spirit accomplishes when we receive Him: "You did not receive the spirit of slavery to fall back into fear, but you have received the Spirit of adoption as sons, by whom we cry, 'Abba! Father!' " (Romans 8:15).

**MAKING CONNECTIONS**

In first-century Palestine, most Israelites' native language was Aramaic. By using "Abba," the Aramaic word for "daddy," Paul is expressing the tender care and love that God has for His people. When God claims us as His children in Baptism, it is not a figurative or coldly intellectual exercise. It is actual and emotional—the love is real, and so is the relationship.

The Holy Spirit, whom we receive in Baptism, gives us "adoption as sons." By that Spirit, we cry, "Abba! Father!" *Abba* is the Aramaic word for "daddy." Paul tells us that in Baptism, we have a relationship with God the Father that is similar to the loving relationship we hope to have with our own human father. But what is best about our relationship with our human father is even better with our heavenly Father. God the Father is every bit as attentive to you as a human father is when he dotes on his baby girl or boy.

But a father who adores his daughter or son is far more understandable to us than a holy and blameless eternal Father who seeks out sinners in love. A daddy's little girl or baby boy is bone of his bone and flesh of his flesh. The father is a human being who is loving someone who came from his own body. With God, it's different. God the Father created all things through the power of His Word (Hebrews 11:3). He is the Giver of life (Romans 4:17). He is the King of the whole world (Psalm 47:7). And in Baptism, He is your Father. He adopts you. He pours out on you the sort of love that only a father can have for his own child. Because of all this, you are royalty. Your Father is the eternal King of an eternal kingdom. You are like Catherine Middleton on her wedding day. If they were capable of sin, the holy angels would probably be tempted to look on you with envy. You are what they can never be. You are a child of God.

**FROM THE BIBLE**

See what kind of love the Father has given to us, that we should be called children of God; and so we are. (1 John 3:1)

**MAKING CONNECTIONS**

While our understanding of God as Father can gain meaning from the framework of earthly fatherhood, it is not dependent on it. Though human fathers often fail in their duties—and some fail more often than they succeed—our heavenly Father never fails us. He is the template of true Fatherhood.

## Let's Hear It for Mommy!

But you don't only have a second Father; you also have a second Mother. In Baptism, God adopts you as His own child by placing you into the care of your new Mother, the Church. Luther writes, "The Spirit has His own congregation in the world, which is the mother that conceives and bears every Christian through God's Word" (LC II 42). It is in and into the Church that a person is baptized. In this way, the Church is our Mother (Galatians 4:23; Revelation 12).

A newly baptized Christian is like a newborn baby in many ways. Newborns are helpless. They depend on their parents (and their mothers in particular) for everything they need. It is from a baby's mother that he or she receives food, warmth, and comfort. It is nuzzled close to his or her mother that a newborn baby feels most safe and most secure. Almost immediately after birth, a baby will sometimes crawl straight to his or her mother's breast. A baby can only see about ten inches at this time. This means that even while a newborn is eating, the child can still see the mother's face. The baby is completely dependent on his or her mother, and this is by God's design.

A newborn Christian also needs his or her Mother. It is from the preaching of the Gospel that the newborn Christian receives the necessary nourishment for his or her faith to strengthen and grow. It is in hearing that Christ has suffered and died for the forgiveness of sins that a Christian receives comfort. There is no better place for a newborn Christian than the place where God promises to feed and care for all His children. Newborn Christians are just as helpless as newborn babies. Satan, the world, and their sinful flesh will still attack them. They need protection. They need food. They need their Mommy.

### Our New Family

Through Baptism, our second birth, we have new parents, and that's wonderful news. We have a Father who makes sure that we always have everything we could possibly need. Because of His great love for us, He entrusts us to the care of our Mother, the Church. In the Church we get to know our new family. We receive support and encouragement from other Christians, and most important, it is in the Church that we get to know our elder Brother.

## Our Brother, Our Keeper

### Of Siblings and Sacrifices

You don't have to go very far in the Bible before you see an example of sibling rivalry. In Genesis 4, the first sons born to Adam and Eve come to God to offer sacrifices to Him. Abel brings a sacrifice from his flock. Cain brings the firstfruits of his crops. Moses writes, "The LORD had regard for Abel and his offering, but for Cain and his offering He had no regard" (Genesis 4:4–5).

God receives Abel's sacrifice because Abel recognizes that sin can only be atoned for with blood. Abel is following the example that God Himself gave when He covered Adam and Eve's iniquity with the skins of animals that He had slain (Genesis 3:21). Moreover, it is Abel's attitude of humility and dependence on God's mercy that

**MAKING CONNECTIONS**

A third-century pastor named Cyprian of Carthage once said that we cannot have God as our Father unless we have the Church as our Mother. There has never been a time in the Church's history that Baptism has not been central to the Church's life.

**FROM THE BIBLE**

Like newborn infants, long for the pure spiritual milk, that by it you may grow up into salvation—if indeed you have tasted that the Lord is good. (1 Peter 2:2–3)

**FROM THE BIBLE**

Therefore be imitators of God, as beloved children. And walk in love, as Christ loved us and gave Himself up for us, a fragrant offering and sacrifice to God. (Ephesians 5:1–2)

makes him capable of giving the proper gift. Cain is different. Instead of offering blood, he offers what he gained from the sweat of his brow. Rather than asking for mercy, he shows off his accomplishments.

Cain offered God the best that he thought he could come up with—the literal fruits of his labors. Because of how much he is personally invested in his offering, Cain is angered that his own works don't gain God's favor. Because of this anger—which is mostly against God—Cain kills his brother. In the very next verse, God confronts Cain directly about his sin, but He does it in a way that gives Cain an opportunity to confess. He asks Cain where Abel is. Cain's reply is filled with the anger against God that led him to kill his brother in the first place. He says, "Am I my brother's keeper?" (Genesis 4:9).

## Big Brother

In Baptism, we all have an elder Brother. We are brought into God the Father's family, a family that already includes a Son. As we say in the Nicene Creed, Jesus is "begotten of His Father before all worlds." He is the eternal Son of the eternal Father. There has never been a time that God the Father has not been Father. There has never been a time that Jesus has not been God's Son. We, on the other hand, are different. We become God's children in a particular place and at a particular time. We are adopted in Baptism.

Our elder Brother is a far better sibling than Cain ever could have been. When Cain was born, Eve thought he was the promised Messiah. She said, "I have gotten a man, the Lord" (Genesis 4:1, author's translation). Cain, however, was a man filled with envy and hate. He was the opposite of what the Lord's Messiah, Jesus, would be. Jesus is our keeper. He guards us against all that would harm us. Because we deserve God the Father's

**TECHNICAL STUFF**

From the very beginning, sin has been atoned for by the shedding of blood. Just after the account of the fall into sin, we read, "And the Lord God made for Adam and for his wife garments of skins and clothed them" (Genesis 3:21). The word used for "clothed" in this passage is used elsewhere to describe atonement for sin. God Himself offers the first sacrifice for sin and clothes Adam and Eve with the skins of the animal.

**FROM THE BIBLE**

[Jesus] is the image of the invisible God, the firstborn of all creation. For by Him all things were created, in heaven and on earth, visible and invisible, whether thrones or dominions or rulers or authorities—all things were created through Him and for Him. (Colossians 1:15–16)

wrath, Jesus took on human flesh to suffer this wrath in our place. We did the crime, but Jesus did the time.

This is why Paul says, "Do you not know that all of us who have been baptized into Christ Jesus were baptized into His death? We were buried therefore with Him by baptism into death, in order that, just as Christ was raised from the dead by the glory of the Father, we too might walk in newness of life" (Romans 6:3–4). Instead of being angry because of the favor that God the Father showers on us, Jesus has become the Lamb who sheds His blood in our place. Jesus is the elder Brother who will stop at nothing to provide for and protect His siblings. He is definitely the kind of Brother you want to have in your family, and in Baptism, He's exactly the kind of Brother you have.

## Heirs of God

Over the years, I've known two estate court judges. Listening to family members squabble over who deserves to get what piece of their parents' estate is not an easy job. Some days, an estate court judge sees more lawyers in that courtroom than heirs. He or she has to listen to all sorts of testimony on the mental state of the deceased person, the validity of previous wills, and whatever else the lawyers come up with to make their arguments. The judge has to spend endless hours studying the will of the person who died to understand as much as possible about what the deceased person wanted to happen with the estate.

Every case an estate court judge hears is different. The personalities, nuances, and circumstances vary. But there are two things that the estate court judges I know have said are *always* the same:

1. The person whose estate is being argued over is dead, and
2. The only way the court can clearly know what the deceased person wanted is if that person wrote a will.

As strange as it may seem, these two facts become very important when we look at what the Bible says about us being in God's family. In Baptism, God gives us the "Spirit of adoption as sons" (Romans 8:15), but it doesn't stop there. Later in the same passage, Paul writes, "The Spirit Himself bears witness with our spirit that we are children of God, and if children, then heirs—heirs of God and fellow heirs with Christ" (vv. 16–17).

When Paul's readers first encountered this passage, their jaws probably dropped to the floor. To be God's heir means that when God dies, you inherit all that is bequeathed to you in His will. But we know from Hebrews 9:17 that "a will takes effect only at death, since it is not in force as long as the one who made it is alive."

**TECHNICAL STUFF**

The Holy Scriptures are divided into two groups of books: the Old Testament and the New Testament. In that context, ***testament*** means "covenant." In the Old Testament, God establishes covenants with His people through Adam and Eve, Noah, Abraham, Isaac, Jacob, Moses, and, finally, David. Taken as a group, these are the old covenant (or testament). The New Testament refers to the books that describe the covenant that Jesus made with us during His earthly ministry: the Lord's Supper.

## The Reading of the Will

We are heirs because we are baptized into Christ, but we receive the inheritance because Christ has died. Just as in the disposition of an earthly estate, we can only know what we are going to inherit if we listen to the reading of the will. Our Lord gave His will on the night before His death when He instituted the Lord's Supper. Luther puts it this way: "[Jesus] said: 'For this is My blood of the new testament, which will be shed for many for the remission of sins. But I tell you I shall not drink again of this fruit of the vine until that day when I drink it new with you in My Father's kingdom.' With these most delightful words He bequeaths to us, not the riches or the glory of the world but once and for all absolutely all blessings, that is, as I have said, the remission of sins and possession of the future kingdom" (AE 29:213).

In Baptism, you are an heir of God. What you inherit is the best thing imaginable: the forgiveness of all your sins and a share in our Lord's own unending life.

# A Priest Forever

In Exodus 19:6, God calls Israel "a kingdom of priests and a holy nation." When He calls His people "priests," He is not saying that all of them will serve in the tabernacle as the Levites do. He is not saying that they will all be pastors. He is saying that because they are His people and bear a physical sign of that relationship through circumcision, they will all act in a priestly way in the world. They will pray for one another and for all people. They will make God's Word the focal and pivot point of their lives. Because God's name has been put on them, they will bear it in the world.

## A Royal Priesthood

In the New Testament, Peter connects this image to Baptism. First, he says, "You have been born again, not of perishable seed but of imperishable" (1 Peter 1:23). Do you see it? "Born again" is Baptism language. It is in and through Baptism that God gives us second birth as His children. This is what Jesus was saying (and

Nicodemus was misunderstanding) in John 3.

From here, Peter launches into an extended description of what it means to be baptized. A few verses into the next chapter, Peter makes the connection to Exodus 19. He says, "You are a chosen race, a royal priesthood, a holy nation, a people for His own possession, that you may proclaim the excellencies of Him who called you out of darkness into His marvelous light. Once you were not a people, but now you are God's people; once you had not received mercy, but now you have received mercy" (1 Peter 2:9–10). In Exodus 19:6, God says that His people will be a "kingdom of priests and a holy nation." Peter's words go a step further than that. In Peter's description, we are still a chosen people. We are still priests. We are still bearing God's name into the world.

But Peter doesn't stop there; he also says that we are royalty. The "kingdom of priests" has become a "royal priesthood." In Baptism, we are heirs of God who continue to pray for the world and bear God's name into it. We know that we will receive all that Jesus has bequeathed to us, and we are filled with a desire to let everyone know that the gift is for them too.

It's good to be a member of the royal family.

**FROM THE BIBLE**

Jesus answered, "Truly, truly, I say to you, unless one is born of water and the Spirit, he cannot enter the kingdom of God." (John 3:5)

# Study Questions

1. What are the two births that Jesus talks about in John 3?

2. What new Father and Mother do we gain through Baptism, and what gifts do they give us?

3. What does it mean to have Jesus as our Brother?

4. What do we inherit through Baptism?

*Visit lutheranism101.com to download the free Leader Guide.*

5. What does it mean to be a priest in the New Testament?

*Visit lutheranism101.com to download the free Leader Guide.*

# Discussion Questions

1. The parents of an expected royal child know the privileges and obligations their child will receive because of that royal status. How is this similar to the situation of Christian parents who know that their child will be baptized—made royal—soon after birth? List the privileges and obligations inherent to earthly royalty, and decide how or if those parallel the privileges and obligations Baptism bequeaths.

2. Christians claim God as our Father, Christ as our Brother, and the Church as our Mother. What are the modern challenges that the Church faces through its use of "family" talk?

*Visit lutheranism101.com to download the free Leader Guide.*

Because of this, some would argue that Christians should avoid using these familial terms in discussing our faith. Why are such terms beneficial and essential to the Church today, especially in difficult situations?

3. How would our lives and our worship practices be different if all Christians were not called to be a royal priesthood?

*Visit lutheranism101.com to download the free Leader Guide.*

CHAPTER 4

# A Bath like No Other

## In This Chapter

- God's Law reveals that we are born sinners, dead in sin.
- Baptism connects us to Jesus' death, and we are cleansed by His blood.
- The amount of water and mode of application do not matter.
- God is the active party in Baptism.

## Church Speak

The Church has its own way of talking. There are words that you'll hear in the Church that you generally won't hear anywhere else. *Baptism* is one of those words. As we've discussed Baptism, we've used other special, churchly words: *sin, Sacrament, Trinity.* When the Church uses a word, it often imports extra meaning into that word that wouldn't be there if the word wasn't being used in the Church. *Baptism* is like that. Outside of the Church, a baptism is just a bath. Nothing more. Nothing less. Not in the Church. In the Church, Baptism is more.

We know that Baptism is a bath that is different from any other bath since in Baptism, the water is combined with God's Word. The water also puts God's name on us. Instead of washing away dirt, Baptism washes away sin. The Lord's gift of Baptism truly is a bath like no other.

So far, we've barely gotten our feet wet, but now it's time to dive headfirst into how the Bible talks about our dirtiness and how Baptism washes it away.

## A Different Sort of Dirt

You've heard the complaint: "There's never any good news in the newspaper!" War, rape, crime, deceit in Washington, floods, tornadoes, terrorist attacks, and even newly discovered ways you're going to be killed by the food you eat and the water you drink—those are the sorts of things we read and hear about every day. The good news, the happy news, the news that might actually bring a smile to your face is buried between two auto dealership ads on page 17. If you blink while you're turning the page, you won't even know it's there.

We like to blame the media for holding back the good news. We imagine that there is a curmudgeonly editor at the top of a building in New York City who blithely uses his power to rain woe, grief, and despair on us all. What we don't want to think about is the fact that the curmudgeonly editor has significant resources devoted to finding out what sorts of stories people want to read. He wants to print those stories so that he can charge a higher premium for advertising. The editor doesn't want to ruin our day; he wants to increase revenue. He sells newspapers so that he can sell advertising. If he thought a story about Sally getting a pony for her birthday would sell lots of ad copy, he'd put it on page 1.

The newspapers—both in print and online—give us what we want. We actually *love* to read about death, war, and famine. We want to read the stories that reveal the sickness of human nature first, and that's why they're usually on the front page. We revel in sickness, disaster, and death. We are addicted to it. Though we'd never admit it, it's why many of us read the news in the first place. And this is nothing new.

## No New News

In the days of Noah, the evil of man was the reason that God brought judgment on the whole world. "The LORD saw that the wickedness of man was great in the earth, and that every intention of the thoughts of his heart was only evil continually" (Genesis 6:5). Man's evil state hasn't changed. David expresses it in almost the same way over a thousand years later: "The LORD looks down from heaven on the children of man, to see if there are any who understand, who seek after God. They have all turned aside; together they have become corrupt; there is none who does good, not even one" (Psalm 14:2–3).

**NEED TO KNOW**

**Original sin:** the sinful state into which human beings are born because of the sin they inherit from Adam.

Our evil and sinful condition doesn't change, because the enduring reality of our existence is that we are sinful. Though sin is not part of the very essence of being human, it is the situation into which all of us are born after the fall. We are born with original sin. Because of this, we are sinful from the moment we first exist as distinct human beings. Sin is the air we breathe. We can never escape it in this life. The reality of our sinfulness puts us into a very bad situation. David put it this way: "For You are not a God who delights in wickedness; evil may not dwell with You. The boastful shall not stand before Your eyes; You hate all evildoers. You destroy those who speak lies; the LORD abhors the bloodthirsty and deceitful man" (Psalm 5:4–6).

**FROM THE BIBLE**

Behold, all souls are Mine; the soul of the father as well as the soul of the son is Mine: the soul who sins shall die. (Ezekiel 18:4)

Not only is sin the ever-present reality from which we can never escape, but in our natural state, we are in absolute opposition to God, and God *hates* all evildoers. Adam and Eve knew this on an instinctual level after their fall into sin. They covered themselves in fig leaves and tried to hide from God. They felt shame for the first time. God was holy, and they were not. They wanted nothing more than to flee from Him.

## Holy Terror

Adam and Eve knew that the holiness of God and the sinfulness of man could not peacefully coexist. But Adam and Eve weren't the only people in the Bible whose sin scared them. Some three thousand years later, Isaiah encountered God in the temple, and because Isaiah was a sinner, he was terrified. He was afraid that when he saw God in the temple, he would die. He said, "Woe is me! For I am lost; for I am a man of unclean lips, and I dwell in the midst of a people of unclean lips; for my eyes have seen the King, the LORD of hosts!" (Isaiah 6:5).

Isaiah was always aware of the serious consequences of his sin. Later, he would write that sin separates us from God so completely that God cannot even hear the prayers of the wicked: "Your iniquities have made a separation between you and your God, and your sins have hidden His face from you so that He does not hear" (Isaiah 59:2).

## Here's the Situation

The only way our situation could be more serious would be if we were already dead and in hell. As it is, this is the natural situation of man:

We do not trust in God (unbelief).

We are in absolute rebellion against God (hard-heartedness).

The Law is written on our hearts, and our hearts know we've violated it (stricken conscience).

There is no way out of the hopeless situation we're in (helplessness).

We either know our situation (despair), or we don't (pride).

Our sinfulness is laid bare by God's Law. When we sin, we often feel the pangs of conscience immediately. God has written His Law on our hearts so that even those people who have never heard of Him still have some checks on their sinful behavior (Romans 2:15). When we hear God's Law as it is revealed to us in the

Scriptures, we learn how desperate our situation is. We learn that there is absolutely no way that we can save ourselves.

## Drowning in Sin

Luther says: "The chief office or force of the Law is to reveal original sin with all its fruit. It shows us how very low our nature has fallen, how we have become utterly corrupted. The Law must tell us that we have no God, that we do not care for God, and that we worship other gods [Romans 3:10–18]—something we would not have believed before and without the Law. In this way, we become terrified, humbled, depressed. We despair and anxiously want help, but see no escape" (SA III II 4).

**FROM THE BIBLE**

For when Gentiles, who do not have the law, by nature do what the law requires, they are a law to themselves, even though they do not have the law. They show that the work of the law is written on their hearts, while their conscience also bears witness, and their conflicting thoughts accuse or even excuse them. (Romans 2:14–15)

When you realize how prideful you are and the full extent of your rebellion against God, it is because the Law is doing its work. There's nothing we can do about our situation. Left on our own, we're sunk. We aren't just drowning; we're already dead. Only one heartbeat separates us from eternal condemnation in hell. That is the situation that Jesus enters with words of comfort. He says, "Whoever believes and is baptized will be saved" (Mark 16:16).

Baptism changes everything. Baptism gives faith, and through that faith, Baptism delivers the forgiveness that Christ won for us on the cross. All of this comes because in Baptism, God gives us a unique sort of bath that cleanses us from a special sort of dirt.

# A Different Sort of Soap

## Liar, Liar . . .

When Isaiah was trembling in fear because he had seen God in His temple, he said that he was a man of "unclean lips." He was saying something very similar to what the writer of Psalm 116 says: "I said in my alarm, 'All mankind are liars' " (v. 11). Isaiah knows his heart. He knows that his words often express the sin that fills him. Because we

**FROM THE BIBLE**

No human being can tame the tongue. It is a restless evil, full of deadly poison. With it we bless our Lord and Father, and with it we curse people who are made in the likeness of God. (James 3:8–9)

**NEED TO KNOW**

**Altar of Incense:** an altar in the Holy Place where incense was perpetually burned in front of the entrance to the Holy of Holies. It was in the Holy of Holies, over the ark of the covenant, that God had promised to be visibly present for the Israelites in the Old Testament. This is why God is often said to be "enthroned on the cherubim" (1 Samuel 4:4; 2 Samuel 6:2; 1 Chronicles 13:6; Psalm 80:1; Psalm 99:1; Isaiah 37:16).

**FROM THE BIBLE**

For the life of the flesh is in the blood, and I have given it for you on the altar to make atonement for your souls, for it is the blood that makes atonement by the life. (Leviticus 17:11)

have completely lost the image of God in the fall, all of our words are tainted. It's difficult for us to speak even the shortest of sentences without lying in some way. Even when we do something simple, like recount a conversation we had earlier in the day, we still tend to color the truth. We come out sounding a bit better than we actually did. The person we were talking to comes out sounding a bit worse.

Our lips are unclean and sinful because they speak what is in our heart. Jesus says, "What comes out of the mouth proceeds from the heart, and this defiles a person" (Matthew 15:18). Isaiah knows all this. He knows that he is a liar, like the rest of humankind, and because of that, he is terrified to be in the presence of God.

## . . . Lips On Fire?

Isaiah's reaction to being in the presence of God makes a lot of sense to us. From what we already know, it's the way we would expect it all to be. What is extraordinary is the way that the angels respond to Isaiah's fear: "Then one of the seraphim flew to me, having in his hand a burning coal that he had taken with tongs from the altar. And he touched my mouth and said: 'Behold, this has touched your lips; your guilt is taken away, and your sin atoned for' " (Isaiah 6:6–7).

The "coal" that the angels took from the altar of incense was either a burning piece of wood or a superheated stone. Incense was perpetually burned on these coals. But it wasn't just incense that found its way to this altar. Each time a sin offering was made, some of the blood from the sacrifice was smeared on the horns of the altar of incense. The coal that purified Isaiah's lips had first been washed with blood.

Isaiah's lips were cleansed with a coal that was only clean because it came from a bloody altar. The blood of that sin offering took away Isaiah's sins. Blood is the spiritual soap of the Bible. If you want to have your sins washed away, blood is the way to do it. Jesus is Himself the final and greatest sin offering of all. John puts it this way: "The blood of Jesus . . . cleanses us from all sin" (1 John 1:7).

## A Bloody Revelation

But how does this bloody talk connect to Baptism? We've already discussed what makes a bath into a Baptism: water and the Word of God. Even though blood doesn't seem to enter that picture, it's actually pivotal. In the Book of Revelation, John is given the gift of seeing reality as it actually is. The word *revelation* means "unveiling." It is as if you are at a reception when a new sculpture is going to be shown to the public for the first time. At first, you only see the vague shape of the sculpture under a sheet. Then, when the sheet is taken off, you see all of the details. You see the hands and the feet. If you look really close, you can even see the marks the chisel made each time it struck the marble. That's what happened for John when the Holy Spirit gave him the vision that he wrote down for us.

At one point in the vision, John gets to see those who have already died and are enjoying eternal bliss in heaven. There are thousands and thousands of people. There are so many that John can't even begin to count them. While John is taking the scene in, one of the elders asks him whom they're seeing. John doesn't know, but he knows that the elder does. He says, "Sir, you know." The elder then describes the multitude: "These are the ones coming out of the great tribulation. They have washed their robes and made them white in the blood of the Lamb. Therefore they are before the throne of God, and serve Him day and night in His temple; and He who sits on the throne will shelter them with His presence. They shall hunger no more, neither thirst anymore; the sun shall not strike them, nor any scorching heat. For the Lamb in the midst of the throne will be their shepherd, and He will guide them to springs of living water, and God will wipe away every tear from their eyes" (Revelation 7:14–17).

## Laundry Time

John speaks in the same way in Revelation as he did in 1 John. The robes are washed and made white with "the blood of the Lamb." This is pretty amazing language. If you looked on the Internet, you could find hundreds of Web pages that would tell you how to get a bloodstain out of your clothes. You probably wouldn't find any that would say how to get a stain out of your clothes *using* blood.

Blood is one of the last things that comes to mind when someone says "laundry detergent." But in this passage, laundry detergent is just what the blood of the Lamb is. It is also no accident that John talks about a Lamb in this text. And in the Bible, Lamb talk is Jesus talk. When Jesus was baptized, John the Baptist proclaimed, "Behold, the Lamb of God, who takes away the sin of the world!" (John 1:29). By using the phrase "Lamb of God" in this passage, the apostle John was bringing to mind the words of John the Baptist and all sorts of Old Testament imagery as well.

**FROM THE BIBLE**

"Worthy is the Lamb who was slain, to receive power and wealth and wisdom and might and honor and glory and blessing!" (Revelation 5:12)

## Passed Over

When God delivered His people from slavery in Egypt, He sent ten plagues against the Egyptians, and the tenth was the worst. In this plague, God sent His angel to slay the firstborn of Egypt, both man and beast. The only way for a family to escape this plague was through blood. They had to sacrifice a lamb, roast it over an open flame, eat it that same night, and then paint the lintel and doorpost of their house with the lamb's blood. When God saw the blood, He would pass over the house and not kill any who lived there (Exodus 12).

**FROM THE BIBLE**

The blood shall be a sign for you, on the houses where you are. And when I see the blood, I will pass over you, and no plague will befall you to destroy you, when I strike the land of Egypt. (Exodus 12:13)

John the Baptist says that Jesus is the Lamb of God who takes away the sins of the world. In the original Passover, God accepted the blood of a lamb instead of pouring out His just wrath on those who lived in the house that was painted with the blood. When Jesus died for us on the cross, God accepted the blood of His own Son—the Lamb of God—instead of pouring out His just wrath on the whole world.

The blood of the Lamb washed away the sins of all people. Jesus was the Lamb for God's household, the whole world (John 3:16). All of the language of Passover is pulled into Revelation when John says, "They have washed their robes and made them white in the blood of the Lamb."

## All Washed Up

The blood of God's own Passover Lamb perfectly cleans the robes of His saints. But what is the washing? When do the robes become white?

We can find the answer by looking at how the most ancient Christians put this text in Revelation into practice. In those days, all people were naked when they were baptized. Before entering the water, people would take off their old clothes.

This was a way of confessing that they were putting off the old sinful nature. In Baptism, we receive new clothes; we are clothed with Christ Himself. Paul says, "For as many of you as were baptized into Christ have put on Christ" (Galatians 3:27). In order to confess what the Scriptures say about Baptism, the one being baptized was always given a new white robe upon coming out of the water.

When a person goes into the water, he or she is dirty, soiled to the core by sin. The person comes out clean, washed with the blood of Christ and clothed with Him. In heaven, we wear the white robes of our Baptism forever. Our robes are washed and made white by the blood of the Lamb. The blood of Jesus is truly the best and only soap for the job.

**MAKING CONNECTIONS**

Receive this white garment to show that you have been clothed with the robe of Christ's righteousness that covers all your sin. So shall you stand without fear before the judgment seat of Christ to receive the inheritance prepared for you from the foundation of the world. (*LSB*, p. 271)

## A Different Way of Getting Wet

Since the essential features of Baptism are water and the Word of God, the amount of water isn't really that important. In a Baptism, a drop of water will do just as well as a river or an entire ocean. So long as the person gets wet and the name of God is combined with the water, the person will be baptized and receive all that God offers through this Sacrament.

**FROM THE BIBLE**

I will sprinkle clean water on you, and you shall be clean from all your uncleannesses, and from all your idols I will cleanse you. (Ezekiel 36:25)

### Just How Wet?

This is a great example of how Baptism is a very different sort of bath. Only in Baptism can a person become completely clean even though he or she is only splashed with a few drops of water; but some Christians would disagree strongly with this statement. They would say that unless someone is immersed, they are not baptized. Christians who think of Baptism this way believe that the Greek word for *baptism* always means "to immerse." Because of this, they would say that the Word of God makes the "mode" of Baptism absolutely clear: in order to be baptized, a person must be completely submerged under the water.

There are two major problems with this approach to Baptism. First, it fails to recognize that God is the one who is active in Baptism, and He can work with a drop of water just as well as He can work with a bathtub full. The second problem is that the Bible uses the word "baptize" for methods of washing other than immersion.

The best example of this second problem is Mark 7:3–4. Here Mark describes some of the ritual customs of the Pharisees: "For the Pharisees and all the Jews do not eat unless they wash their hands properly, holding to the tradition of the elders, and when they come from the marketplace, they do not eat unless they wash. And there are many other traditions that they observe, such as the washing of cups and pots and copper vessels and dining couches." Mark says that the Pharisees wash—in Greek, the word is *baptize*—dining couches. No Jewish home would have had the cisterns, pulleys, and manpower necessary to immerse a dining couch before each and every meal. Clearly, Mark has something other than total immersion in mind when he uses the word "baptize."

**MAKING CONNECTIONS**

The amount of water doesn't matter, but the one giving it does. Alluding to Baptism in John 4:14, Jesus says, "Whoever drinks of the water that I will give him will never be thirsty again. The water that I will give him will become in him a spring of water welling up to eternal life."

## Quantities May Vary

We also know from Early Church history that the amount of water used for a Baptism could vary. An extremely early Christian document called the Didache says that though it is wonderful if you can baptize in running water (like a river), it is not necessary. The Didache recommends that the person performing the Baptism use whatever water he has available. It doesn't matter whether it's a little or a lot (Didache, Chapter VII).

Baptism is truly a different sort of bath. You can get clean with just a drop of water or with several gallons. You can be barely wet or completely soaked. The amount of water doesn't matter at all. What is most important is that the water is combined with God's Word and administered according to His command.

**NEED TO KNOW**

**Baptismal shell:** Either a real shell or made of precious metal, the baptismal shell may be used to apply water in Holy Baptism. Much early Christian artwork depicts Baptism using a cup or shell. For example, Jesus' Baptism, He is shown standing in the river, and John is using a shell to scoop water and baptize Jesus.

## A Different Sort of Clean

One of the most important passages in the Bible about Baptism is 1 Peter 3:18–21. In verse 21, Peter says, "Baptism . . . now saves you." What a clear statement of what God does in Baptism! Unfortunately, the statement is a scandal to many Christians. Those who don't understand what God promises and does through Baptism can't seem to wrap their heads around this straightforward statement. They think Peter must have been exaggerating. He must have meant something else. He couldn't possibly intend the words to say what they say.

The saddest consequence of this uneasiness is that most Bible translations try to soften Peter's language to one extent or another. As a result, they render his words into English in a way that allows them to ignore the baptismal implications.

This makes life difficult for those of us who rejoice in what Peter is saying. How can we share this passage with our friends and relatives when the translators try to make it less clear and less forceful than it was when Peter first wrote it? Because of these difficulties, I have done my best to translate the passage in a way that doesn't shy away from anything that Peter says.

### Peter's Baptismal Proclamation

"For Christ also suffered once for sins, the righteous for the unrighteous, that He might bring you to God, having been put to death in the flesh but made alive in the Spirit in whom also He preached to the spirits in prison after He went [to them], because when God's patience waited in the days of Noah they did not obey while the ark was being prepared, in which a few, that is, eight souls, were saved through water. Baptism, which is the antitype, now saves you, not as a removal of dirt from flesh but as a plea to God for a good conscience through the resurrection of Jesus Christ" (1 Peter 3:18–21, author's translation).

Peter begins and ends with Jesus' resurrection. Baptism connects us to our Lord's death and resurrection, and after Jesus' resurrection, the first thing that He did was to descend into hell and preach about His victory over death to those who were there. When Peter describes this event, he specifically mentions those who had disobeyed in the days of Noah. Because of the sinful rebellion

**TECHNICAL STUFF**

In 1 Peter 3:21, we hear that Baptism is an antitype. The words ***type*** and ***antitype*** are used in the Bible to refer to events, people, and objects in the Old Testament that have a fuller and clearer expression in the New Testament. What happens in the Old Testament is the type, and what happens in the New Testament is the antitype. In this passage, God's act of saving Noah and his family is the type, and God's act of saving us through Baptism is the antitype.

**FROM THE BIBLE**

Let us draw near with a true heart in full assurance of faith, with our hearts sprinkled clean from an evil conscience and our bodies washed with pure water. (Hebrews 10:22)

of the whole world, at that time the whole Christian Church on earth was eight people: Noah, his wife, his three sons, and their wives.

When Peter mentions Noah and the flood, he cannot help but tie it to Baptism. Just as the flood wiped out millions of evildoers in the days of Noah while at the same time saving Noah and his family, so also Baptism drowns our sinful flesh and saves us. The particular gift that Peter connects to the salvation we receive in Baptism is a "good conscience." A good conscience is an enormous gift.

### A Good Conscience

We've all faced difficult decisions. Sometimes it seems like whatever choice we make, our consciences are going to be troubled. This outcome is far too common. However, on rare occasions, our struggle with such a decision will lead to a positive outcome. We weigh all that we know about the situation and make a choice with confidence. In those rare circumstances, we say to ourselves, "I made that decision with a clear conscience."

But as you know, our consciences usually don't stay clear for long. Things don't go exactly as we expected. We find out that we didn't really navigate the decision as well as we thought. Our consciences are pricked, even though we are sure that we made the very best choice possible. We can never get free of nagging doubts—and often for good reason.

Baptism is a plea to God for a good conscience, a plea answered by the fact that Baptism unites us with Christ in His death and resurrection. What goes for Jesus now goes for us. In Baptism we now have a life that cannot be taken away, and we have a conscience that is as clear as Jesus' conscience. The gift of a good conscience can only come to us through the forgiveness of sins. When we are forgiven, our consciences feel clean because the sins that accuse them are gone. That's a different kind of clean than we can get from any other sort of bath!

## A Different Sort of Washer

On the night before Jesus died on the cross, He did something that should have boggled His disciples' minds. He laid aside His outer garments, tied a towel around His waist, knelt before the disciples, and began to wash their feet. Washing someone's feet wasn't just a menial task; it was a slave's task. After a person traveled down the dirty, dung-covered streets of the ancient world, his sandal-clad feet were often coated with filth. The wealthy had slaves who would wash their feet when they came inside. The poor did it themselves. What happened on this night was something that no one would have ever imagined. A master never washed his slaves' feet.

## Socially Unconventional

The social conventions didn't matter to Jesus. He was and is the Creator and Master of the whole universe. When Jesus arrived on that Thursday night to eat the Passover with His disciples, He could have asked any one of them to wash *His* feet, the feet of the eternal King of the universe. No one deserved to receive a foot washing more than Jesus.

**FROM THE BIBLE**

For even the Son of Man came not to be served but to serve, and to give His life as a ransom for many. (Mark 10:45)

But our Lord freely takes on the role of the most menial slave. He washes His disciples' feet, and the disciples are understandably confused. Peter said what most of the disciples were probably thinking: "You shall never wash my feet" (John 13:8a). Peter knows that what Jesus is doing goes against every custom that existed in the ancient world. He doesn't want to be party to such a scandalous event. But Jesus insists. He says, "If I do not wash you, you have no share with Me" (v. 13:8b). In this passage, Jesus is talking to Peter and Peter alone. The Greek of this passage even uses a singular form of the word *you* to make it absolutely clear to whom Jesus is talking. So is that all there is to this story? Is this simply a record of a historical event that happened in first-century Jerusalem, or is there something we can learn from it?

## Pointing the Way

When our Lord washes His disciples' feet, He is pointing them forward to the gift of Baptism that He will institute less than two months later. All of the New Testament's language of washing is tied up in the gift of Baptism. In some cases the connection is obvious, and in others it is subtler. In this passage, we find the connection in the Lord's own words: "If I do not wash you, you have no share with Me."

Those particular words of Jesus bring us into the story. In Baptism, Jesus washes *us*. This is one of the most important ways that Baptism is a bath unlike any other. Remember Eustace in chapter 1? He thought he could get rid of his dragon skin on his own, but he couldn't. Aslan had to do it. We are in the same situation. We cannot get clean on our own. We could literally scrub our skin off completely, and the sin would remain. If Jesus does not wash us, we have no part with Him.

It is often hard for us to see Baptism this way. When a person is baptized, there are always at least two people involved. First, there's the one being baptized. Second, there's the one who is getting that person wet and saying the words. I've seen dozens of baptisms and performed several myself, and I'll be the first to admit that I've never seen Jesus pour the water or say the words at a Baptism.

**MAKING CONNECTIONS**

Often a baptismal candle is lit from the paschal candle and given to the newly baptized. Baptismal candles may be used for special celebrations, especially baptismal birthdays. "Receive this burning light to show that you have received Christ who is the Light of the world. Live always in the light of Christ, and be ever watchful for His coming, that you may meet Him with joy and enter with Him into the marriage feast of the Lamb in His kingdom, which shall have no end" (*LSB*, p. 271).

## It Wasn't Me

When I baptized my daughter, I said, "I baptize you in the name of the Father and of the Son and of the Holy Spirit. Amen." While I said "Father," "Son," and "Holy Spirit," I scooped water out of the font with a gold-plated baptismal shell and poured it on her forehead three times. She screamed each time the water splashed on her face. After she was baptized, I wiped my daughter's forehead with a baptismal cloth and lit a candle that confessed the faith that God had just granted her.

To everyone who was gathered there, I seemed to be the one doing everything. I breathed in the air that my larynx converted into the words I was speaking. The muscles in my hand and arm scooped up the water out of the font and poured it on my daughter's head. I looked at her with my own eyes while I was doing it so I could be sure that I actually poured the water onto her and not somewhere else. I was very present in that moment. My role in the Baptism was significant and essential. Someone had to actually pour the water and say the words. I didn't actually lay eyes on Jesus that morning.

But Jesus was there the whole time. Jesus made the water. It was His words I was speaking. It was His name I was pouring with the water onto my daughter's forehead. Baptism gives all of the gifts that we've been talking about because God does

**FROM THE BIBLE**

Therefore, we are ambassadors for Christ, God making His appeal through us. (2 Corinthians 5:20)

the washing. It has the power to give the gifts because Jesus has instituted Baptism in order to shower us with them.

On the day of my daughter's Baptism, my hands did the work, but Jesus was using them. My lips moved, but Jesus was speaking His words. My daughter was being baptized, but Jesus was bringing her into His family. When Jesus washes you, you have a part with Him, and that makes Baptism a bath like no other.

# Study Questions

1. Why was Isaiah's terror in the presence of the Lord justified?

   What did the angel do to take care of Isaiah's problem, and how is this solution relevant for us?

2. Compare and contrast Baptism with an ordinary bath in the following areas:

   Dirt

   Soap

*Visit lutheranism101.com to download the free Leader Guide.*

The Washer

3. In Greek, *Baptism* means "bath," and it clearly is one. How is it different from other baths in its execution and its effects, and why is this so important?

*Visit lutheranism101.com to download the free Leader Guide.*

# Discussion Questions

1. What does the distinction between Baptism and other sorts of baths tell us about God?

2. Although God calls people to faith through His Word as well, Baptism is the particular Means of Grace through which God makes us His children, marking us as His own. In His omnipotence, God could have chosen to accomplish His purposes in another way or even through Word alone. Why do you think God uses Baptism for this purpose? What is it about the form and content of this Sacrament that makes it the perfect choice?

PUTTING IT ALL TOGETHER

# Luther's Flood Prayer

Martin Luther wrote a prayer for his revision of the baptismal liturgy (1523 and 1526) called the *Sindflutagebett*—the Flood Prayer. Luther's inclusion of the Flood Prayer brings an element of catechesis to the rite through the narrative. Luther places before those gathered at the font the watery witness of God's mercy delivered in water in both the Old Testament and the New Testament. The prayer recalls the floodwaters sent by God to destroy the earth and the merciful rescue of Noah and his family, who were borne in the safety of the ark upon those same waters. It retells the story of the exodus and how the waters that parted to allow the Israelites to escape Egypt and cross the Red Sea in safety were the waters that drowned their pursuers. And it calls to mind the Baptism of Jesus in the Jordan River.

"Almighty and eternal God, according to Your strict judgment You condemned the unbelieving world through the flood, yet according to Your great mercy You preserved believing Noah and his family, eight souls in all. You drowned heart-hearted Pharaoh and all his host in the Red Sea, yet led Your people Israel through the water on dry ground, foreshadowing this washing of Your Holy Baptism. Through the Baptism in the Jordan of Your beloved Son, our Lord Jesus Christ, You sanctified and instituted all waters to be a blessed flood and a lavish washing away of sin.

"We pray that You would behold name(s) according to Your boundless mercy and bless him/her/them with true faith by the Holy Spirit, that through this saving flood all sin in him/her/them, which has been inherited from Adam and which he himself/she herself/they themselves has/have committed since, would be drowned and die. Grant that he/she/they be kept safe and secure in the holy ark of the Christian Church, being separated from the multitude of unbelievers and serving Your name at all times with a fervent spirit and a joyful hope, so that, with all believers in Your promise, he/she/they would be declared worthy of eternal life; through Jesus Christ, our Lord." (Prayer text from *LSB*, pp. 268–69.)

# PART THREE

## What you'll learn about:

- There is only one God over all, one Baptism for the forgiveness of sins, and one undivided Church to which all Christians belong.
- In Baptism, the Holy Spirit is both giver of gifts and the gift Himself.
- Christ received a sinner's Baptism so that we might receive the righteous Baptism of our Lord.
- Combined, the water and God's Word are mighty to do His will when used as Christ has directed.
- The Bible is packed with stories of water that remind us of Baptism, but not every watery incident should be interpreted as a baptismal symbol.

# How Can Baptism Do It?

It seems impossible. A few drops of water and God's triune name hardly seem like enough to work such wonders. Yet through a simple act, the Holy Spirit fills our hearts with countless gifts and immeasurable mercy. He does this by tying our Baptism to the cross of Christ, where cleansing blood was spilled for the sins of the world.

CHAPTER 5

# The Gift of the Holy Spirit

## In This Chapter

- There is only one Lord, one Baptism, and one Body of Christ.
- The Holy Spirit is both the gift and the giver.
- Christ was baptized into our sin; we are baptized into His righteousness.
- Through Baptism, the Holy Spirit works our rebirth and renewal.

## Whose Baptism Is It Anyway?

When I was in junior high, I attended a Pentecostal church for about a year. There were many things that this church didn't understand about what the Bible teaches, but Baptism was one of the places where they were most confused. I had been raised a Lutheran and had begun confirmation classes before I started attending this church. I knew a little bit about what God had done for me at my Baptism when I was less than a month old. I thought of my Baptism as something that was real and had enduring value in my life.

Whenever I talked about my Baptism, the members of the Pentecostal church gave me uncomfortable looks. They'd never heard anyone talk the way I was talking. They were convinced that you needed to consciously ask for Baptism. They believed it was something you did for God and that those who thought that Baptism saved them were taking credit for their own salvation.

**BELIEVE, TEACH, CONFESS**

Baptism is not a work that we offer to God. It is a work in which God baptizes us. In other words, a minister baptizes us on God's behalf. God here offers and presents the forgiveness of sins, and so forth, according to the promise "Whoever believes and is baptized will be saved" (Mark 16:16). (Ap XXIV 18)

**NEED TO KNOW**

to be the supernatural ability to speak in heavenly languages (ecstatic speech), and that this ability is a sign that you have received the gift of the Holy Spirit. In the New Testament, every example of speaking in tongues refers to speaking in an understandable human language.

## Does It Really Count?

My Pentecostal friends believed there were two baptisms and that I'd received neither of them. The first baptism was water baptism, and it only counted if you asked for it and already had faith in Christ before you received it. The second was baptism of the Holy Spirit. When the Pentecostals spoke of "Holy Spirit baptism," they always referred to the various outpourings of the Holy Spirit in the Book of Acts. They thought that Holy Spirit baptism was accomplished through the laying on of hands and that it was always accompanied by what they called "speaking in tongues."

I wanted to believe that my new friends knew what they were talking about, so I let them try to give me this baptism of the Holy Spirit that they liked to talk about. They laid hands on me, prayed, and asked the Holy Spirit to come on me. They had told me that when the Holy Spirit came, He would move me to speak in a heavenly language, but it never happened. They tried for over an hour on several occasions, but I never spoke in tongues. To them, this demonstrated very clearly that I was a "mere believer" and not a "true Christian."

**NEED TO KNOW**

**Holy Spirit baptism:** the teaching among some Christians that the Holy Spirit is given apart from the water Baptism that Christ instituted in Matthew 28:19.

**MAKING CONNECTIONS**

The idea that "speaking in tongues" refers to the ability to speak in a heavenly language not understood by man is a very recent development in Christian thought. When Luther uses the term, he reflects the older, scriptural teaching when he writes about the custom in his day of reading the Gospel lesson in Latin: "Hence has come the custom in all lands, to read the gospel immediately before the sermon in Latin, which St. Paul calls speaking in tongues in the congregation" (AE 40:142).

## How Do We Know?

The time that I spent among the Pentecostals was troubling. A group of sincere Christians whom I trusted had said that if I had received the gift of the Holy Spirit, I would speak in tongues, and I never did. This raised serious questions for me.

Was I really a Christian?

If I was a Christian, why didn't I have the Holy Spirit?

If my Baptism when I was a baby hadn't done anything, did I need to be baptized again?

After about a year among the Pentecostals, I returned to my parents' church. After three years of patient instruction from my pastor, I was finally able to answer all of these questions, and I began to appreciate again all that God had done for me in my Baptism.

Whether you have ever faced those questions or not, exploring the passages in Scripture that provide the answers will enrich your understanding of one of the greatest gifts Christ gives through the waters of Holy Baptism: His Spirit.

## One Lord, One Faith, One Baptism

When my Pentecostal friends suggest that there are two baptisms taught in Scripture, they usually start with John 3:5. Jesus says, "Truly, truly, I say to you, unless one is born of water and the Spirit, he cannot enter the kingdom of God." They say that Jesus was referring to two births, two baptisms. They say that one is of water, and the other is of the Spirit.

There are two ways we can respond to this from our Lord's own words. The first is to note that the word "born" only appears once. "Of water" and of "the Spirit" are two ways to describe the one birth. The second is to see the phrase "water and the Spirit" as an example of *hendiadys*, a literary device that shows up fairly often in the Bible. Sometimes when two words in the Bible are connected by the word *and*, one word is modifying the other. The first place this happens is in Genesis 1:2, where Moses describes the earth as "without form *and* void" (emphasis added). Because of this literary device, the phrase in Genesis is often translated as "formless void." When it comes to Baptism in John 3:5, the same sort of thing is going on. "Water and the Spirit" means something like "Spirit-water." Luther expresses this thought clearly when in the Small Catechism he says that Baptism is "the water included in God's command and combined with God's word" (SC IV 1).

But we don't have to rely on just our understanding of the literary device in John 3. Elsewhere in Scripture, we learn that there is only one Baptism for Christians. Paul talks about this very issue when he explains how we are called to be Christians. He says, "There is one body and one Spirit—just as you were called to the one hope that belongs to your call—one Lord, one faith, one baptism, one God and Father of all, who is over all and through all and in all" (Ephesians 4:4–6).

**MAKING CONNECTIONS**

And I believe in one holy Christian and apostolic Church,

I acknowledge one Baptism for the remission of sins,

and I look for the resurrection of the dead

and the life of the world to come. Amen. (*LSB*, p. 191)

## There Can Be Only One

Because we receive the name of God in Baptism and through it He claims us as His own children, there can be only one Baptism. We have the name of one God upon us. We are born into one Body—the Holy Church. We have one divine Father. We have one hope of everlasting life.

If we listen carefully to what Paul is saying, we will notice that if we change the number in one place, we have to change it in all of the places it shows up. If "one Baptism" becomes "two Baptisms," then we must also have two Bodies, two Spirits, two Lords, two faiths, and two Gods and Fathers of all. Paul's entire argument in Ephesians rests on the fact that in each of these cases there is *one and only one* thing being confessed.

> **FROM THE BIBLE**
>
> Now you are the body of Christ and individually members of it. (1 Corinthians 12:27)

## A Body Double

Though my Pentecostal friends would have been mortified to hear it, by splitting Baptism in two, they were falling into idolatry. As Christians, we confess that there is one God who subsists in three persons: the Father, the Son, and the Holy Spirit. These three show up in Paul's statement: one Spirit, one Lord (Jesus, God the Son), and one Father. If each of these three is not one but two, then we have two Trinities—two Gods. As bad as that way of thinking is, there is a subtler way in which the "two Baptisms" theology leads us into even more dangerous idolatry. Changing "one" to "two" gives us two Gods, but it also gives us two Bodies.

When the Bible describes the Church as the Body of Christ, it is saying several important things. First, the Bible is saying that all Christians live in a perfect unity that is itself a gift of God because all are members of Christ's Body. The ways we distinguish ourselves from one another in our culture have no place in the Church. Paul expresses this idea in a passage we looked at in chapter 4: "For as many of you as were baptized into Christ have put on Christ. There is neither Jew nor Greek, there is neither slave nor free, there is no male and female, for you are all one in Christ Jesus" (Galatians 3:27–28). Second, the Bible says that Christ is not the God of the dead, but of the living (Matthew 22:32). The Church is alive and draws its life from Christ Himself.

Distinguishing between water baptism and baptism of the Holy Spirit cuts the Body of Christ in half, and most Pentecostals will freely admit this even though they almost never explore all of the implications. The way that my Pentecostal friends distinguished between the two bodies was to refer to the first group as "mere believers" and the second as "true Christians" or "Spirit-filled Christians."

Because I was never able to speak in a heavenly language, my Pentecostal friends believed that I had never passed from the first group to the second. They said I wasn't willing to allow the Holy Spirit to completely control me. Because of my resistance to the Spirit's work, they claimed I would never be able to live the sort of victorious Christian life that they thought they were living.

## Preach It, Paul!

The way my Pentecostal friends were speaking is very different from what we hear from Paul. When Paul says that all class distinctions are irrelevant when it comes to being part of the Body of Christ, he means it. In the Church, a king has no greater standing before God than a slave. A pastor has no greater spiritual standing than a baby who was baptized just a few seconds ago.

But if it really is contrary to Scripture to distinguish between water baptism and baptism of the Holy Spirit, what then does Peter mean when he says that we receive the Holy Spirit in Baptism?

## "You Will Receive the Gift of the Holy Spirit"

Think back to Peter's sermon on Pentecost. Then remember that this feast was celebrated every year on the fiftieth day after Passover, and like Passover, Pentecost was a festival that all observant Jews were required to travel to Jerusalem to celebrate. In the year that Jesus suffered, died, and rose again, Pentecost was also the day that God poured out His Holy Spirit upon the Christian Church. It was clear that something amazing was happening when

**MAKING CONNECTIONS**

Paul consistently connects faith and the Holy Spirit. When a person suggests that another does not have the gift of the Holy Spirit, he or she is saying that the other person is not a Christian at all. "May the God of hope fill you with all joy and peace in believing, so that by the power of the Holy Spirit you may abound in hope" (Romans 15:13).

**TECHNICAL STUFF**

Pentecost, or the Feast of Weeks, was established by God when He gave the Law to Moses on Sinai. "You shall observe the Feast of Weeks, the firstfruits of wheat harvest, and the Feast of Ingathering at the year's end. Three times in the year shall all your males appear before the LORD God, the God of Israel. For I will cast out nations before you and enlarge your borders; no one shall covet your land, when you go up to appear before the LORD your God three times in the year" (Exodus 34:22–24).

tongues of fire rested on the apostles. In addition to the spectacle of the fire, all of those who listened to the apostles as they preached heard them speaking in their own languages. The supernatural gift of tongues was given to the apostles so that they could preach the Gospel to all who were gathered. It was not a gift that was intended to reveal that they were "true Christians." The state of our hearts is always hidden. No Christian can ever know whether another person has faith in Christ or not on the basis of what they can or cannot do.

After the miracles of fire and tongues, Peter preached a sermon to the people. In this sermon, he told them about what Jesus had done just fifty days before to win eternal life and salvation for them. Many of those who were gathered believed the word of God that Peter preached. They asked him, "What shall we do?" (Acts 2:37). Peter's reply explicitly connects Baptism with the gift of the Holy Spirit: "Repent and be baptized every one of you in the name of Jesus Christ for the forgiveness of your sins, and you will receive the gift of the Holy Spirit" (v. 38).

**MAKING CONNECTIONS**

It is in Baptism that, like Jesus, we are anointed with the Holy Spirit. The Spirit gives Himself as a pledge that all God's promises to us in Christ are true. "For all the promises of God find their Yes in Him. That is why it is through Him that we utter our Amen to God for His glory. And it is God who establishes us with you in Christ, and has anointed us, and who has also put His seal on us and given us His Spirit in our hearts as a guarantee" (2 Corinthians 1:20–22).

## The Gift

But what, exactly, is the gift of the Holy Spirit? Part of the problem in answering this question is in the way that Peter expresses it. The phrase "gift of the Holy Spirit" can mean two different things. It can mean either "the gift that the Holy Spirit gives" or "the Holy Spirit given as a gift." A careful reading of the rest of the New Testament reveals the answer. It is yes. In Baptism, we receive the Holy Spirit, and in Baptism, it is the Holy Spirit who gives all the gifts.

In the same way He calls, gathers, enlightens, and sanctifies the whole Christian church on earth, and keeps it with Jesus Christ in the one true faith.

In this Christian church He daily and richly forgives all my sins and the sins of all believers.

**BELIEVE, TEACH, CONFESS**

I believe that I cannot by my own reason or strength believe in Jesus Christ, my Lord, or come to Him; but the Holy Spirit has called me by the Gospel, enlightened me with His gifts, sanctified and kept me in the true faith. (SC II, Third Article)

**BELIEVE, TEACH, CONFESS**

This is most certainly true. (SC II, Third Article)

The gifts that we receive with the Spirit are the same gifts that we already know come in and through Baptism. "For in one Spirit we were all baptized into one body—Jews or Greeks, slaves or free—and all were made to drink of one Spirit" (1 Corinthians 12:13). The Holy Spirit unites us into one spiritual Body and in one faith (Ephesians 4:4–6). The Holy Spirit is the way God pours His love into us (Romans 5:5). The Holy Spirit makes us holy (Romans 15:16), gives us the voice to confess that Christ is our Savior (1 Corinthians 12:3), and guards our hearts and minds against false teaching (2 Timothy 1:13–14). Finally, the Holy Spirit does all of these things through the Word, which He has given for the strengthening of our faith and the delivery of all His gifts (2 Peter 1:21).

On the Last Day He will raise me and all the dead, and give eternal life to me and all believers in Christ.

## The Giver

Theologian Norman Nagel expresses these realities this way: "The Holy Spirit is confessed as the giver of gifts. . . . Forgiveness is the all-inclusive gift of the Holy Spirit" ("The Spirit's Gifts in the Confessions and in Corinth." *Concordia Journal*, vol. 18 [3]: 233–34). When Dr. Nagel says this, he is really just expressing something that we can also find in Luther: "The Holy Spirit always has some reason to continue His work in us through the Word. He must daily administer forgiveness until we reach the life to come. At that time there will be no more forgiveness, but only perfectly pure and holy people" (LC II 58).

The Holy Spirit is one of the greatest gifts that we receive in Baptism, and it shouldn't surprise us at all that we receive such a tremendous gift. But if it's so amazing, why shouldn't it surprise us? It shouldn't surprise us because we are not the first people to receive the gift of the Holy Spirit in Baptism. If we want to find the first time the Holy Spirit was given in Baptism, we have to go back three years before Jesus instituted the Baptism that we receive. The place is the Jordan River, and the time is the very beginning of our Lord's ministry.

# What Does He Think He's Doing?

John the Baptist was the true wild man of the New Testament. He dressed like a hippy without decent fashion sense, and he didn't care whom he offended when he preached. If John the Baptist were standing in one of our pulpits, we probably wouldn't put up with him for very long.

But John didn't have a pulpit or a building that the people could kick him out of. He had a river. John set up shop in the Jordan and preached the same message to all who came to him. He preached a "baptism of repentance for the forgiveness of sins" (Mark 1:4; Luke 3:3). John didn't pull punches. He used the strongest language he could come up with to condemn the sins of those who came to him. On one occasion, he said, "You brood of vipers! Who warned you to flee from the wrath to come?" (Luke 3:7). Because of John's unyielding approach, he was eventually put in prison and then executed for preaching against Herod Antipas's sin. Herod had enticed his sister-in-law to divorce his brother and marry him instead.

John's less-than-winsome approach didn't keep the people away. Throughout his ministry, the multitudes kept coming. They knew that John was a prophet. They knew they were sinners. They knew that their sin deserved the condemnation that John was preaching. As Mark wrote, "John appeared, baptizing in the wilderness and proclaiming a baptism of repentance for the forgiveness of sins. And all the country of Judea and all Jerusalem were going out to him and were being baptized by him in the river Jordan, confessing their sins" (Mark 1:4–5).

## Surprise!

Even John was taken by surprise when Jesus showed up to be baptized. That sort of gathering was no place for Jesus. Jesus is the eternal Son of God. He is holy and sinless. He committed no iniquity. He transgressed none of His Father's commands, had no sins to wash away, and had no need of forgiveness. He had no evil of which to repent.

But Jesus came anyway. He walked into the water along with all of the sinners who were coming from Jerusalem and the Judean countryside. Jesus made no distinction between Himself and sinful humanity. He came to receive the same Baptism, the same washing, the same bath as everyone else.

**MAKING CONNECTIONS**

[Jesus'] baptism is a vicarious death for sinners. (Scaer, p. 39)

## Righteous Dude

John recognized Jesus and realized how strange His presence was. He said, "I need to be baptized by You, and do You come to me?" (Matthew 3:14). John knew that he was every bit as sinful as the ones he had baptized. When Jesus came, John wanted his Lord to wash *him*, but Jesus had come to receive a sinner's Baptism. Jesus said, "Let it be so now, for thus it is fitting for us to fulfill all righteousness" (v. 15).

Our Lord's words are very important for several reasons. When we read the accounts of John's preaching and the Baptism that he administered in the Jordan,

**MAKING CONNECTIONS**

Jesus receives the Spirit at John's baptism, and after His life, death, and resurrection gives that Spirit to the church in Baptism. In receiving John's baptism, Christ transforms it into the Baptism of the Holy Spirit. Jesus thereby establishes a continuity between the baptism of John and the one He gives the church. (Scaer, p. 104)

we see many similarities with the Baptism that Jesus would later institute before His ascension. John's Baptism is described as a "baptism of repentance for the forgiveness of sins" (Mark 1:4). These words are similar to what Peter would say about the Baptism that Jesus instituted after His resurrection: "Repent and be baptized every one of you in the name of Jesus Christ for the forgiveness of your sins, and you will receive the gift of the Holy Spirit" (Acts 2:38).

But there is a key difference between John's baptism and the Baptism that Jesus institutes after His resurrection. The difference is that John's Baptism is before the cross and empty tomb, and Jesus' Baptism follows them. John is a transitional figure in every way. He is the final and greatest of the Old Testament prophets. He is also the only one of these Old Testament prophets who sees Jesus come in the flesh. John spends his entire ministry pointing forward to Jesus. His preaching and his Baptism both do this.

## Baptismal Bridge

The bridge between John's Baptism and Jesus' Baptism is the Lord Himself. By submitting to John's Baptism, Jesus fulfills it. Jesus takes into His own body all of the sins that John's Baptism washed from the multitudes. It is because Jesus does this that John can truly say, "Behold, the Lamb of God, who takes away the sin of the world!" (John 1:29).

By "takes away," John means "takes up" or "carries." Jesus picks up all the filth that has been washed away. By submitting to a Baptism that is for sinners, Jesus takes the sin that the sinners lost. Jesus carries those sins in His own body, along with every other sin in human history. He takes them all to the cross.

## Showing Us How It's Done

In Jesus' Baptism we also are given a wonderful picture of our own Baptism. After John baptizes Jesus, Matthew continues the story: "When Jesus was baptized, immediately He went up from the water, and behold, the heavens were opened to Him, and He saw the Spirit of God descending like a dove and coming to rest on Him; and behold, a voice from heaven said, 'This is My beloved Son, with whom I am well pleased' " (Matthew 3:16–17).

Did you catch it? Do you see how Jesus' Baptism by John points forward to our own? When our Lord is baptized, the heavens open and the Holy Spirit descends in the form of a dove and remains on Him. Jesus is the man who is God. Jesus' flesh gets wet in His Baptism, just like our flesh gets wet in ours. He is baptized to fulfill all righteousness; He submits to the waters in obedience to His Father's command. We receive Baptism out of obedience to the command Jesus gives shortly before His ascension. Jesus receives the gift of the Holy Spirit in His Baptism, and we receive the gift of the Holy Spirit in ours.

When the Spirit comes to Jesus, it rests on Him. It stays there. Later, on the cross, "[Jesus] said, 'It is finished,' and He bowed His head and gave up His spirit" (John 19:30). After Jesus accomplishes the salvation of the whole world, it pleases Him to hand over His Spirit to the Church in a little Pentecost. He gives the same Spirit to us in our Baptisms that He received in His. This is the great glory of our Lord's Baptism. It is through it that our Baptisms receive their power. It is through our Lord's own Baptism that we receive the same gift that He received: the Holy Spirit and all His manifold gifts.

## Washing of Regeneration

One passage that Luther uses in the Small Catechism to describe the gifts God gives through Baptism highlights the Holy Spirit's role in that work. "[God] saved us through the washing of rebirth and renewal by the Holy Spirit, whom He poured out on us generously through Jesus Christ our Savior, so that, having been justified by His grace, we might become heirs having the hope of eternal life" (Titus 3:5–7, NIV).

When Paul writes that Baptism is a washing of rebirth (see chapter 3) and renewal, he says that it is the Holy Spirit who accomplishes the rebirth—other translations say "regeneration"—and the renewal. He also says that in Baptism, the Holy Spirit is "poured out on us generously." If we consider what Baptism is and how the Holy Spirit promises to work in the world, we find that it would really be inconceivable for Baptism to do anything but give the Holy Spirit.

Baptism is what it is because the water is combined with the Word of God according to

**MAKING CONNECTIONS**

A child which is to be born two years from now is still nonexistent. At present the maiden who is to carry and bear the child is still unmarried. The child which is to be born of her is nothing and can do nothing. Everyone must admit that one can do nothing until one has life. Therefore all works, however precious and fine they may be, are absolutely nothing if performed before regeneration; they are nothing but sin and death. (AE 22:278)

Christ's institution. But without the Holy Spirit, there would be no Word of God to be combined with the baptismal waters. The Holy Spirit is the author of all Scripture. Whenever God speaks, the Holy Spirit is speaking. He literally breathes out Scripture (2 Timothy 3:16). In fact, in both the Old and New Testaments, the words used for "breath" and "breathing" have the same basic root as the word used for "the Holy Spirit." When the authors of Holy Scripture wrote, they did so as the Holy Spirit directed them (2 Peter 1:21).

## The Giver Who Keeps On Giving

The Holy Spirit gives us new birth by adopting us into God's family. "For you did not receive the spirit of slavery to fall back into fear, but you have received the Spirit of adoption as sons, by whom we cry, 'Abba! Father!' The Spirit Himself bears witness with our spirit that we are children of God" (Romans 8:15–16).

The Holy Spirit is truly the giver of all good gifts. He is the one who delivers to Christians all that Christ won for them by His atoning death on the cross. He is the one who speaks whenever the Word of God is proclaimed. And the Word of God is proclaimed for us in no way that is more sure and certain than when it is preached in the act of Holy Baptism.

# Water Is Water . . . Is Baptism?

**Anabaptist:** One who baptizes "again." Anabaptists rejected infant Baptism at the time of the Reformation and were termed "radical" for this and other views that contradicted traditional Christian and Bible teaching.

**John the Baptist:** Also known as John the Baptizer; prepared the way of the Lord; was a prophet like Elijah of old; baptized Jesus in the Jordan, preaching a Baptism of repentance for the forgiveness of sins. John was a relative of Jesus, son of Zechariah and Elizabeth; he was beheaded by Herod Antipas at the request of his niece.

**Baptist:** An individual, congregation, or church body that usually teaches adult immersion, baptizes as a mark of one's dedication to Christ and new life of faith, and usually terms Baptism an "ordinance" instead of a "sacrament." In addition, Baptism in a Baptist context is usually seen as the work of the Christian rather than God's work. Baptismal regeneration is usually denied.

**Baptismal regeneration:** In Holy Baptism, the Lord promises you the forgiveness of sins and the gift of the Holy Spirit. In theological language, this is "baptismal regeneration." Although the Bible clearly teaches it, many (Reformed) Christians still deny it. Peter had a perfect opportunity to answer the "What shall we do?" question by inviting everyone forward for an "altar call." Instead, he invited them to Baptism.

—From *Lutheranism 101*, p. 137

# Baptized for Forgiveness

But now behold how glorious a thing Baptism is, also how sublime a spectacle Christ's Baptism presented. The heavens opened, the Father's voice was heard, and the Holy Spirit descended, not as a phantom but in the form and figure of a natural dove. Nor was the Father's voice an illusion when He pronounced these words from heaven: "This is My beloved Son; with Him I am well pleased." These were real, natural, human words. And this dove, in the form of which the Holy Spirit was seen, was real and natural. Nevertheless, it was the Holy Spirit. All this was done in honor and praise of the Sacrament of Holy Baptism; for this is not a human institution but something sublime and holy. Eminent personages are involved in it: the Father, who bestows and who speaks here; the Son, who receives and is baptized; the Holy Spirit, who hovers above and reveals Himself in the form of a dove. And the celestial choir of all the angels is present; these skip and dance for joy over this act. Furthermore, the entire heaven stands ajar. If Baptism were a human act and institution, such scenes would not be enacted here. . . .

Since Baptism is a divine act in which God Himself participates and since it is attended by the three exalted Persons of the Godhead, it must be prized and honored. One must agree that Baptism was not invented by any man but was instituted by God. It is not plain water but has God's Word in it and with it; and this transforms such water into a soul bath and into a bath of rejuvenation. . . .

Christ, of course, accepts John's Baptism of water, but He adds the fire. That is, He imparts the Holy Spirit, who kindles His virtues in us. And thus our Baptism in Christ, in which He gives us remission of sin, baptizing us with the Holy Spirit and with forgiveness, remains and continues to be effective. We receive the forgiveness from the Lamb, who bears the sin of the world. But on account of the old Adam we are also baptized for repentance. We must constantly repent; we must constantly mortify our flesh. That is, we must continually mend our evil ways and be cleansed and at the same time always hope for that forgiveness of sin which we now have. When we are baptized and believe in Christ, we do all this. For our Baptism is not, as John's was, one that points to Him who is to bring forgiveness of sin; but our Baptism is Christ's Baptism, which has already brought forgiveness.

(Excerpted from AE 22:173–74, 179–80)

# Study Questions

1. How many baptisms did Jesus institute?

2. What is the "all-inclusive gift of the Holy Spirit"?

3. What does the word *regeneration* mean in its biblical context (Titus 3)?

4. What does Jesus accomplish for us by being baptized?

*Visit lutheranism101.com to download the free Leader Guide.*

5. What would be a good way to answer someone who distinguishes between "water baptism" and "baptism of the Holy Spirit"?

*Visit lutheranism101.com to download the free Leader Guide.*

# Discussion Questions

1. There are dangers in exposing young Christians to the teachings of other faiths, and even of other Christian church bodies. However, there are also dangers in not exposing or, at least, instructing them. What are the plusses and minuses of seeing and learning what other Christians believe and do?

2. Why did John need to come first? He and Jesus were nearly the same age, so why didn't he and Jesus start preaching and baptizing together, essentially team teaching?

*Visit lutheranism101.com to download the free Leader Guide.*

CHAPTER 6

# Water and the Word of God

## In This Chapter

- Baptismal water is powerful when used with God's Word, as Christ has directed.
- The Bible abounds with watery baptismal imagery.
- Not every biblical use of water is an image of Baptism.

## Water Power

"Water and the Word of God"—Lutherans love to describe Baptism this way, and the reason should be obvious: the combination of water with God's Word makes ordinary water into baptismal water.

In his Small Catechism, Luther asked and answered a question that many Christians also ask: "How can water do such great things?" It's an important question because God's use of water in Baptism can cause a lot of confusion. Looking at the water that is actually used is the first step to answering several practical questions about that water:

Does the water itself have special power to give all that God offers in Baptism?

Does the water need to be blessed before it is used in Baptism?

Does water that has been used in Baptism have other special powers?

Is it okay to use water to remind yourself of your Baptism?

Discussing the water of Baptism then leads us to take a closer look at water in the Word of God. God frequently uses water as an image of His saving activity. We, in turn, rejoice that God has always used the stuff of creation to deliver His gifts of life and salvation to sinners like you and me.

## The Water of Baptism

### Holy Water

When we hear the phrase "holy water," Baptism is usually not the first thing that comes to mind. Until I got to college, I didn't know anything about holy water except that it seemed to keep vampires away—and I didn't even know why it did that. When I began to learn more about what other Christians believe, I found out that the reason holy water was part of the vampire legend was because in Roman Catholic churches, water is regularly blessed by priests and bishops so that it can be set aside for holy use. Roman Catholics will sometimes take holy water home and use it in lots of interesting ways. They will water plants with it in their gardens, they will add it to soup, or they will sprinkle it in their bedrooms. Though official Roman Catholic teaching says that the water's actual purpose is to remind a person of his or her Baptism (which is a *good* thing), lots of superstitions have grown up around the concept of "holy water."

**MAKING CONNECTIONS**

In 1 Peter 2:9, we learn that a "holy nation" is a "people for [God's] own possession." Though the entire universe belongs to Him, God has specifically chosen Israel to be His own. That is what makes them holy. When God chooses to use water to adopt someone into His family, then and only then the water is holy as well. It belongs to God and accomplishes His purposes.

At the time of the Reformation, some theologians believed that once water was blessed and set aside for holy use, there was something innate in the water that made it able to do all of the things that Baptism does. The water had been given special, divine power.

When you think about that, the superstitions that surround holy water make a little sense. If the water were endowed with special powers, it would be a great way to fight off vampires. Making your garden grow bigger heads of cabbage would be no problem. And of course, it would be useful for protecting your home against evil spirits. But there is actually nothing special about the water used in Baptism. Most pastors get the water for Baptism out of the same faucet they use to do dishes.

### Simple Water

Responding to theologians who thought the water used in Baptism had a special power that made the water alone able to do all that Baptism does, Luther wrote, "The water is water, in no wise better in quality than that which a cow drinks. But we maintain that to the simple water the Word of promise has been added (Mark 16:16): 'He that believes and is baptized will be saved'; likewise (John 3:5): 'Man must be born again of water and the Spirit' " (AE 1:228).

To avoid misunderstanding, most Lutherans do not use water that has been specially blessed for Baptism. It is entirely unnecessary to bless water ahead of time. One of the prayers Luther wrote for use in the baptismal rite confesses this: "Through the Baptism in the Jordan of Your beloved Son, our Lord Jesus Christ, You sanctified and instituted all waters to be a blessed flood and a lavish washing away of sin" (*LSB*, p. 269). According to Luther, Christ's Baptism in the Jordan blessed all water and made it all appropriate for use in Holy Baptism.

Does this mean that it would be wrong to pray over water and set it aside for holy use? Of course not! Paul writes, "For everything created by God is good, and nothing is to be rejected if it is received with thanksgiving, for it is made holy by the word of God and prayer" (1 Timothy 4:4–5). It is always appropriate to set aside something we use in church by reading the Word of God and asking our Lord for His blessing. However, in the case of the water used for Baptism, it is not necessary to say anything except what the Lord Himself has given us to say: "I baptize you in the name of the Father, and of the Son, and of the Holy Spirit." Those are the words by which Jesus Himself instituted Baptism. They are the words that combine the water with God's Word and place upon the person's own brow the very name of God.

**FROM THE BIBLE**

For as the rain and the snow come down from heaven and do not return there but water the earth, making it bring forth and sprout, giving seed to the sower and bread to the eater, so shall My word be that goes out from My mouth; it shall not return to Me empty, but it shall accomplish that which I purpose, and shall succeed in the thing for which I sent it. (Isaiah 55:10–11)

## Respect, Not Superstition

Even though Lutherans do not think of baptismal water as a superstitiously magical holy water, people still wonder if there's anything special or different about water that has been used in a Baptism. Since the water of Baptism has been combined with the Word of God, some wonder if after the Baptism, the water has special powers. The answer is no. The water stays united with the Word of God only at the time that it is combined with the Word of God and is being used according to Christ's mandate. After the Baptism has been accomplished, the water's holy purpose is complete. It is no different from any other water.

Still, it is a good idea to dispose of water that has been used for a holy purpose in a reverent way. Many churches have a special sink called a *piscina* that drains directly into the ground. It is normally used to reverently dispose of the Lord's blood after a Communion service. It is also appropriate to use it to dispose of baptismal water. If a piscina is not available, it is best to pour the water directly onto the ground.

**BELIEVE, TEACH, CONFESS**

In the morning when you get up, make the sign of the holy cross and say:

In the name of the Father and of the † Son and of the Holy Spirit. Amen.

(SC, Daily Prayers)

## A Good Sign

Sometimes you might enter a church that has its baptismal font near the entrance to the nave. You may see people dipping their fingers in the font and making the sign of the cross as they enter. If you've never seen this before, it can seem a bit strange. You might wonder whether or not it's appropriate to use the water or make the sign of the cross. Don't worry! The answer is that you are completely free. In *Lutheran Service Book*, the following instruction is printed in many of the places where the pastor makes the sign of the cross: "The sign of the cross ☩ may be made by all in remembrance of their Baptism" (*LSB*, p. 167).

It is appropriate for any Christians to make the sign of the cross whenever they want to rejoice in the many gifts God gave them in Baptism. If water is helpful to you, you are free to use it or not. The freedom you have to make that choice is another of the gifts God gives in and through Baptism.

# Water in the Word

Water is a big part of our lives. Most of us encounter water within a few minutes of getting up. Water is in the tub. Water is in the coffee machine. Water is even in the air! When we drive to work, there's water keeping our windshield clean and there's water keeping the engine cool. When we pay our bills, water is one we're careful to always pay on time. Nobody wants to be around people who haven't had running water in their house for a few days.

**FROM THE BIBLE**

He gathers the waters of the sea as a heap; He puts the deeps in storehouses. (Psalm 33:7)

God has carefully permeated our everyday existence with water. We can't imagine what life would be like without it. In fact, without water, there'd be no life at all. Without water, I couldn't have written this book, and you wouldn't be reading it.

## Water, Water, Everywhere

It should come as no surprise, then, that water is also big in the Bible. Just two verses into the Scriptures, we hear, "The Spirit of God was hovering over the face of the waters" (Genesis 1:2). The world starts as a ball of water. God makes a separation between the waters above (the blue sky) and the waters below (the blue seas). Next, God gathers the water to one place and lets dry land appear. As we continue to move through that first chapter of Genesis, we get more and more water. There are seas (v. 10). There is mist watering the ground. Because of that mist, there's even water involved when God forms Adam from the dust of the ground (Genesis 2:5–7).

Throughout the whole Bible, water is the stuff of life and death. It destroys all the wickedness on the earth in the flood while at the same time saving Noah and his family in the ark (Genesis 6–8). Pharaoh uses water to murder God's people when he tosses their baby boys into the Nile (Exodus 1), and God uses water to save His people when He brings them through the Red Sea on dry ground and then literally pours out His wrath on Pharaoh's army (Exodus 14–15). The farther you get in the Bible, the wetter you get.

**FROM THE BIBLE**

Then Moses and the people of Israel sang this song to the LORD, saying, "I will sing to the LORD, for He has triumphed gloriously; the horse and his rider He has thrown into the sea." (Exodus 15:1)

## Even More Water

When God establishes the way He will be worshiped in the Old Testament, He commands the Levites to wash themselves with water before they offer sacrifices for the sins of Israel (Exodus 40:12). Later, the prophet Elisha tells a pagan foreigner that water is what God is going to use to cleanse him from his leprosy (2 Kings 5). There's no doubt about it. God loves to use water to accomplish His gracious purposes. But what are we to make of all this biblical water? Should we immediately think of Baptism every time God does something special with water?

**FROM THE BIBLE**

So [Naaman] went down and dipped himself seven times in the Jordan, according to the word of the man of God, and his flesh was restored like the flesh of a little child, and he was clean. (2 Kings 5:14)

Consider first that the main purpose of Scripture is to tell us in detail how God has answered the problem of our sinfulness. John summarizes this purpose toward the end of his Gospel: "These [words] are written so that you may believe that Jesus is the Christ, the Son of God, and that by believing you may have life in His name" (John 20:31).

In the first few chapters of the Bible, we hear how God created the universe and gave it to Adam and Eve as a gift. Adam and Eve were created perfect. They loved and trusted God for all things. In the fall, Adam and Eve rebelled against God and brought His holy wrath upon themselves. All of this is covered in three chapters. In the rest of the Bible (1,186 chapters), we learn about how God has saved all people from their sins. This culminates in what Jesus did for us on the cross, but in the Old Testament, there are many places where God saves His people in clear and decisive ways. Many involve water, and two of these "wet" high points are even mentioned in the New Testament. By exploring these images of Baptism, we'll better understand how to think of other watery passages not specifically talked about in the New Testament.

## The Flood

Before the flood, things were bad. Almost no one remembered the promise of salvation that God had given to Eve on the day of the fall. Most people were living according to the extremely wicked and selfish intents of their hearts, with no regard for God and His revelation that had been passed down by the patriarchs for ten generations.

It shouldn't surprise us that things went so wrong. What *is* surprising is that God waited so long to show the full extent of His wrath against sin. By the time God sent the floodwaters, some sixteen hundred years had passed since the fall into sin. And even after God decided to blot out man from the earth, He still waited one hundred twenty years before sending the rain. God waited even though things were so bad that "the LORD regretted that He had made man on the earth, and it grieved Him to His heart" (Genesis 6:6). He gave time for Noah to build and preach. He gave time for the animals to enter the ark. He gave time for the people of the world to repent.

> **FROM THE BIBLE**
>
> The LORD saw that the wickedness of man was great in the earth, and that every intention of the thoughts of his heart was only evil continually. And the LORD regretted that He had made man on the earth, and it grieved Him to His heart. (Genesis 6:5–6)

## Wrath and Mercy

Finally, all of the animals were safe on the ark along with Noah, his wife, his three sons, and their wives. God was ready to show the surpassing greatness of both His wrath and His mercy. On that day of judgment, God shut the door of the ark and then opened the floodgates of the heavens and the earth. Many died. Eight lived. Wrath and mercy were bound together on that day through one common element: water.

Noah and his family were saved by water at the same time that the rest of the world was killed by it. Luther says in the Flood Prayer: "According to Your strict judgment You condemned the unbelieving world through the flood, yet according to Your great mercy You preserved believing Noah and his family, eight souls in all" (*LSB*, p. 268). Luther connects Baptism with the flood in his prayer because Peter does the same thing when he talks about how Baptism saves us (1 Peter 3:20–21).

## A Foreshadowing Flood

Even though Baptism is not mentioned by name anywhere in the Old Testament, we are not reading into Scripture when we say that God's judgment of the world in the flood is a picture of what God does in Baptism. In fact, there are a number of things we can learn about Baptism by thinking about it in terms of the flood. Here are three of them:

God is active in Baptism just as He was active in the flood.

In Baptism, God drowns the sinner and gives life to the saint, just as in the flood, He drowned the wicked and saved those who believed in Him.

Baptism washes away our sin just as the waters of the flood cleansed the earth of its wickedness.

It is no mistake that God saves Noah and his family through the same waters that He uses to judge the world. God already knew about the gift of Baptism that He was going to give. He wanted His people to have stories in their hearts and minds that would help them understand all of the wonders of the gift they would later receive.

**NEED TO KNOW**

**Israelites:** the descendants of Jacob, son of Isaac. Because Jacob was also called Israel, his descendants are often called Israelites.

## Let My People Go!

It didn't take long after the flood for things to get bad again, even in Noah's own family (Genesis 9:20–27). By the time a thousand years had passed, evil was as rampant in some parts of the world as it had been when God sent the flood in the first place. Egypt was one of those places, and that's where God's chosen people, the descendants of Jacob, were living. Pharaoh, the king of Egypt, had enslaved the Israelites, but there were so many of them that Pharaoh was afraid of a slave uprising. In order to reduce Israel's population, he ordered that all male Israelite babies be drowned in the Nile.

Because of their great suffering, the people of Israel cried out to God for deliverance. God chose Moses to proclaim His word to Pharaoh and command him to let the Israelites go. Pharaoh refused to obey God until God sent ten plagues on Egypt, the last of which claimed Pharaoh's own child. Finally, Pharaoh let the Israelites go.

## Crossing the Red Sea

Even after all the horrible plagues, Pharaoh soon regretted his decision. Because of this, Pharaoh sent his army after the Israelites. Moving quickly, Pharaoh's army penned in the Israelites on one side, and the shore of the Red Sea was on the other. It looked as if the Israelites' escape from Egypt was going to meet a bloody and tragic end. But God was faithful to His people. He sent a pillar of cloud between the Israelites and the army and parted the Red Sea with a strong east wind.

The Israelites passed through the sea in safety! They walked on dry ground with walls of water on their right and left. Pharaoh's army pursued them, and after the Israelites had arrived safely on the other side, God drowned all of Pharaoh's host in the sea. Afterward, Moses, Aaron, and Miriam sang a song of praise to God for His great victory: "I will sing to the Lord, for He has triumphed gloriously; the horse and his rider He has thrown into the sea" (Exodus 15:1).

**FROM THE BIBLE**

And the Lord went before them by day in a pillar of cloud to lead them along the way, and by night in a pillar of fire to give them light, that they might travel by day and by night. (Exodus 13:21)

The crossing of the Red Sea is filled to the brim with baptismal imagery. It is similar but not identical to what we already saw in the account of the flood. Paul compares the crossing of the Red Sea to Baptism in 1 Corinthians 10:1–4: "For I do not want you to be unaware, brothers, that our fathers were all under the cloud, and all passed through the sea, and all were baptized into Moses in the cloud and in the sea, and all ate the same spiritual food, and all drank the same spiritual drink. For they drank from the spiritual Rock that followed them, and the Rock was Christ."

## Helpless but Not Hopeless

The pillar of cloud was the place where God made His gracious presence visible for Israel. The cloud protected them from Pharaoh's army as the Red Sea parted. Then, it continued to lead them throughout their wilderness wanderings for forty years! Like Baptism, the pillar of cloud said, "You are Mine. I will watch over you. I will protect you. I will fight for you against your enemies." There's one other interesting thing to note about clouds. They are made . . . of water.

Israel's crossing of the Red Sea brings to mind many of the ideas already explored in connection with the flood. The water that brought salvation to the Israelites brought judgment to the Egyptians. Also God acted unilaterally when He saved the Israelites at the Red Sea. The people were completely helpless. None of them were soldiers, and they were facing a battle-hardened army. They may not have had a single weapon. God was the only one who could turn certain death into the promise of new life.

We see in the crossing of the Red Sea the same helplessness that is our state before God washes us in the waters of Baptism. The Israelites recognized this. Because of their appreciation for the great salvation God had worked for them against Egypt, the exodus became the primary way that the Old Testament people of God spoke of their redemption.

## Still More Water

As much as we can learn about Baptism by considering the stories of the flood and the Red Sea, you are probably thinking, "But there's more, isn't there?" These two stories only account for about five chapters in the Old Testament, and there are over nine hundred other chapters to look at. Surely some of these talk about water. Surely some of these are about Baptism.

Absolutely! There are other stories the Church has often looked at to enhance her understanding of Baptism. There are many places in the Old Testament where you can see God connecting water with the salvation He works for His people. There are many verses that talk about water cleansing a person from sin. There are many Old Testament passages that use imagery that is very similar to the way the New Testament speaks about Baptism.

But there are also passages in the Old Testament where water is just water. When Abraham fills a skin with water as he sends Hagar and Ishmael away, it probably doesn't have anything to do with Baptism. Abraham just doesn't want them to get thirsty (Genesis 21:14). When Elisha commands the people of Judah to attack the Moabites and stop up their wells (2 Kings 3:18–19), his words probably have a lot more to do with military tactics than with anything in the New Testament.

## Sidetrack or Symbol?

If you want to appreciate the depths of the baptismal imagery that fill the Scriptures, that's absolutely wonderful. It's always good to keep Baptism in mind as you read about all that God has done for you in Christ. But sometimes water is just water. If you don't see a clear way in which the passage is connecting water to God's saving activity, then the passage is probably not about Baptism. If your reading of the passage would lead you to say something about Baptism that is not explicitly taught in a clear passage of Scripture, you should be careful to not jump to conclusions.

But if God is really saving someone through water, then go for it. Rejoice in the fact that God uses the Old Testament to increase our appreciation of what He does in the New Testament. When Elisha tells Naaman that if he dips himself in the Jordan seven times, he will be healed of his leprosy (2 Kings 5), there's nothing wrong with letting that passage remind you of how God has cleansed you through the waters of Holy Baptism. When the Spirit is hovering over the water in Genesis 1, there's nothing wrong with remembering that God the Holy Spirit creates faith out of nothing by allowing Himself to be delivered in the baptismal waters.

**FROM THE BIBLE**

In the beginning, God created the heavens and the earth. The earth was without form and void, and darkness was over the face of the deep. And the Spirit of God was hovering over the face of the waters. (Genesis 1:1–2)

Water. Word. Baptism. Those three words can add a lot of joy to the way you read the Scriptures, and there's absolutely *nothing* wrong with that!

# Study Questions

1. How is the water of Baptism the same as all other water?

2. How is the water of Baptism different from all other water?

3. Is it okay to make the sign of the cross over yourself? What is the meaning of such an action?

4. How can the stories of the flood and the crossing of the Red Sea help us understand water imagery in the Bible?

*Visit lutheranism101.com to download the free Leader Guide.*

# Discussion Questions

1. List some of the ways you encounter water on a daily basis. How can many of these encounters remind you of what God does through water and His Word in Baptism?

2. Read the story of Naaman in 2 Kings 5. What are some parallels between the water in this story and the water of Holy Baptism?

PUTTING IT ALL TOGETHER

# The Order of Service

## Holy Baptism

Let's look at the baptismal rite commonly used in the Lutheran Church. The wording of the service of Holy Baptism is located on the left side of the page; a brief commentary is on the right. It is good to familiarize yourself with this rite so you can understand what will happen and can ask your pastor about any sections that may not be clear to you. (See *LSB*, pp. 268–71.)

---

An appropriate baptismal hymn may be sung. The candidate(s), sponsors, and family gather with the pastor at the entrance of the nave or at the font.

When candidates are unable to speak for themselves, the sponsors answer the questions on their behalf.

Stand

P In the name of the Father and of the ☩ Son and of the Holy Spirit.

Matthew 28:19b

C **Amen.**

### The Invocation

We call upon the triune God at the onset of worship to bless that which will follow and to confess the true God to whom we direct our worship. The trinitarian invocation also recalls our Baptism. We call on the Father, Son, and Holy Spirit, in whose name we are baptized. "For through Him we both have access in one Spirit to the Father" (Ephesians 2:18).

Here at the beginning of the rite, the use of the Invocation recognizes that the Baptism that will follow is done "in the name of," that is, by the authority of the Holy Trinity. Baptism, whether of a child or an adult, is not the pastor's work; it is the Lord's work being done through the pastor.

P Dearly beloved, Christ our Lord says in the last chapter of Matthew, "All authority in heaven and on earth has been given to Me. Therefore go and make disciples of all nations, baptizing them in the name of the Father and of the Son and of the Holy Spirit." In the last chapter of Mark our Lord promises, "Whoever believes and is baptized will be saved." And the apostle Peter has written, "Baptism now saves you."

Matthew 28:18b–19; Mark 16:16a; 1 Peter 3:21

The Word of God also teaches that we are all conceived and born sinful and are under the power of the devil until Christ claims us as His own. We would be lost forever unless delivered from sin, death, and everlasting condemnation. But the Father of all mercy and grace has sent His Son Jesus Christ, who atoned for the sin of the whole world, that whoever believes in Him should not perish but have eternal life.

## The Baptismal Address

This address presents the Scripture's account of the Lord's institution of Holy Baptism. It then proclaims Baptism's benefits: namely, the one beiing baptized will be made a disciple of the Lord and will receive the salvation Christ worked for him or her on the cross. This our greatest need, for all are born sinful and separated from God. Here, in Baptism, Christ claims the one being baptized as His own, so he or she will be delivered from sin, death, and eternal condemnation.

The pastor addresses each candidate:

P How are you named?

R Name

## Giving of the Name

A name is important. Parents spent a lot of time selecting the perfect name. Perhaps it is a family name, a biblical one, or one with a certain meaning. This Christian name, a person's first and middle names, will be used throughout the baptismal rite. This is significant, for God says to His children, "Fear not, for I have redeemed you; I have called you by name, you are Mine" (Isaiah 43:1).

The pastor makes the sign of the holy cross upon the forehead and heart of each candidate while saying:

P Name, receive the sign of the holy cross both upon your ☩ forehead and upon your ☩ heart to mark you as one redeemed by Christ the crucified.

## Giving of the Sign of the Cross

This is an ancient ceremony associated with Holy Baptism. It signifies that the benefits of Christ's cross are being given to your child through this sacrament. The sign of the cross becomes the possession of the baptized. He or she may wish to make the sign of the cross by tracing it upon the body. With that body language, the Christian is confessing the baptismal faith and remembering the blessings received in the Sacrament. The baptized child of God often make the sign of the cross before prayer when rising in the morning, when going to sleep at night, and in times of trouble. Another appropriate time to use the sign is whenever the pastor blesses the baptized.

**P** Let us pray.
Almighty and eternal God,
according to Your strict judgment You condemned the unbelieving world through the flood,
yet according to Your great mercy You preserved believing Noah and his family, eight souls in all.
You drowned hard-hearted Pharaoh and all his host in the Red Sea,
yet led Your people Israel through the water on dry ground, foreshadowing this washing of Your Holy Baptism.
Through the Baptism in the Jordan of Your beloved Son, our Lord Jesus Christ,
You sanctified and instituted all waters to be a blessed flood and a lavish washing away of sin.

We pray that You would behold _name(s)_ according to Your boundless mercy
and bless _him/her/them_ with true faith by the Holy Spirit,
that through this saving flood all sin in _him/her/them_,
which has been inherited from Adam
and which _he himself / she herself / they themselves has/have_ committed since,
would be drowned and die.
**Grant that _he/she/they_ be kept safe and secure in the holy ark of the Christian Church,**
being separated from the multitude of unbelievers
and serving Your name at all times with a fervent spirit and a joyful hope,
so that, with all believers in Your promise,
_he/she/they_ would be declared worthy of eternal life;
through Jesus Christ, our Lord.

**C** **Amen.**

If the sponsors were previously enrolled, the service continues below with the Holy Gospel.

## Prayer

This prayer is taken from Martin Luther's baptismal rite and has commonly been called the "Flood Prayer." It recounts baptismal imagery from the Old Testament and our Lord's own Baptism. Wonderful in their own right, the Old Testament accounts also foreshadow the greater saving flood that the one being baptized will encounter in Holy Baptism. These waters will wash away all sin that is inherited and every sin that is committed. The baptized will be placed, safe and secure, in the ark of the Christian Church. This prayer petitions the Lord to make his or her Baptism a saving act, in accordance with His promise.

P From ancient times the Church has observed the custom of appointing sponsors for baptismal candidates and catechumens. In the Evangelical Lutheran Church sponsors are to confess the faith expressed in the Apostles' Creed and taught in the Small Catechism. They are, whenever possible, to witness the Baptism of those they sponsor. They are to pray for them, support them in their ongoing instruction and nurture in the Christian faith, and encourage them toward the faithful reception of the Lord's Supper. They are at all times to be examples to them of the holy life of faith in Christ and love for the neighbor.

The pastor addresses the sponsors.

P Is it your intention to serve __name of candidate(s)__ as sponsors in the Christian faith?

R *Yes, with the help of God.*

P God enable you both to will and to do this faithful and loving work and with His grace fulfill what we are unable to do.

C **Amen.**

## Address to Sponsors

IBaptism makes new members for the family—the Holy Christian Church. This means the members of the Church are now siblings. Because these brothers and sisters have an interest in their new sibling, sponsors are usually assigned, especially at he baptism of a child. These sponsors are representatives of the Church and are asked to support and encourage the parents in the ongoing nurture of the baptized. If necessary, the sponsors act as parental substitutes attending to the faith of the baptized, should the child lose his or her parents. For this reason, the selection of sponsors should be made with great care. It is most fitting for the sponsors to be selected from among the faithful of the congregation. At the least, the sponsors should believe and confess the faith into which the child is baptized. In this section, the sponsors state their intention to serve the baptized in this way.

P Hear the Holy Gospel according to St. Mark.

They brought young children to [Jesus] that He might touch them; but the disciples rebuked those who brought them. But when Jesus saw it, He was greatly displeased and said to them, "Let the little children come to Me, and do not forbid them; for of such is the kingdom of God. Assuredly, I say to you, whoever does not receive the kingdom of God as a little child will by no means enter it." And He took them up in His arms, put His hands on them, and blessed them.

Mark 10:13–16 NKJV

P This is the Word of the Lord.

C **Thanks be to God.**

## Gospel Reading

This Gospel reading is St. Mark's account of Jesus' blessing the little children. Jesus says that whoever does not receive the Kingdom as a little child will by no means enter it. A little child earns nothing. Whatever he or she has is a gift; nothing is gained for himself. Young or old, everyone receives the Kingdom in the same way—as a little child—only as a gift. So it is with the blessings that Baptism brings. Baptism is all God's work, not the work of the baptized. It is pure gift. This Gospel is read to emphasize the gifting nature of Baptism.

The pastor places his hands on the head(s) of the candidate(s), and the congregation joins in praying:

C **Our Father who art in heaven,**
**hallowed be Thy name,**
**Thy kingdom come,**
**Thy will be done on earth as it is in heaven;**
**give us this day our daily bread;**
**and forgive us our trespasses as we forgive those who trespass against us;**
**and lead us not into temptation,**
**but deliver us from evil.**

**Matthew 6:9–13**

**For Thine is the kingdom and the power and the glory forever and ever. Amen.**

If the baptismal party has stood at the entrance of the nave to this point, they now move to the font. A hymn may be sung during the procession. Then the pastor says:

P The Lord preserve your coming in and your going out from this time forth and even ☩ forevermore.

C **Amen.**

## The Lord's Prayer

When faith speaks, it prays. Jesus gave us the Lord's Prayer in response to His disciples' plea of "teach us how to pray." It is the family prayer of the Christian Church. In Holy Baptism, the one being baptized is made a child of God. Now he or she is privileged to call God "Father." In fact, the Small Catechism reminds us that the words "Our Father who art in heaven" mean that "God tenderly invites us to believe that He is our true Father and that we are His true children, so that with all boldness and confidence we may ask Him as dear children ask their dear father" (SC III).

Sit

The pastor addresses the candidate(s) and asks the following questions:

P ___Name(s)___, do you renounce the devil?

R *Yes, I renounce him.*

P Do you renounce all his works?

R *Yes, I renounce them.*

P Do you renounce all his ways?

R *Yes, I renounce them.*

P Do you believe in God, the Father Almighty, maker of heaven and earth?

R *Yes, I believe.*

## Renunciation of the Devil/Confession of the Apostles' Creed

The faith into which one is being baptized is confessed in the Apostles' Creed. The devil, the enemy of God, is renounced, as is his lordship over the life of the baptized. The one to be baptized is being brought under new ownership—that of the Holy Trinity. If he or she is too young to articulate the faith, the parents, along with the sponsors and/or congregation, will speak in his or her stead. This is the confession in which all Christians are called.

**P** Do you believe in Jesus Christ, His only Son, our Lord, who was conceived by the Holy Spirit, born of the virgin Mary, suffered under Pontius Pilate, was crucified, died and was buried; He descended into hell; the third day He rose again from the dead; He ascended into heaven and sits at the right hand of God the Father Almighty; from thence He will come to judge the living and the dead?

**R** *Yes, I believe.*

**P** Do you believe in the Holy Spirit, the holy Christian Church, the communion of saints, the forgiveness of sins, the resurrection of the body, and the life everlasting?

**R** *Yes, I believe.*

**P** _Name_, do you desire to be baptized?

**R** *Yes, I do.*

The pastor pours water three times on the head of each candidate while saying:

**P** _Name_, I baptize you in the name of the Father and of the Son and of the Holy Spirit.

**C** **Amen.**

The pastor places his hands on the head of the newly baptized while saying:

**P** The almighty God and Father of our Lord Jesus Christ, who has given you the new birth of water and of the Spirit and has forgiven you all your sins, strengthen you with His grace to life ☩ everlasting.

**C** **Amen.**

## The Baptism

With the application of the water and the invoking of the name comes the actual Baptism. Here the one to be baptized receives the new birth and all the blessings the Lord has promised to attach to this washing.

The pastor may place a white garment on the newly baptized while saying:

P Receive this white garment to show that you have been clothed with the robe of Christ's righteousness that covers all your sin. So shall you stand without fear before the judgment seat of Christ to receive the inheritance prepared for you from the foundation of the world.

## White Garment

In Baptism the newly baptized has "put on Christ" (Galatians 3:27); that is, he or she has been covered with the righteousness of Christ. He or she is now a co-heir with Christ of His glory. A white garment may be given to signify this reality.

The pastor may light a baptismal candle from the paschal candle and give it to the newly baptized while saying:

P Receive this burning light to show that you have received Christ who is the Light of the world. Live always in the light of Christ, and be ever watchful for His coming, that you may meet Him with joy and enter with Him into the marriage feast of the Lamb in His kingdom, which shall have no end.

## Candle

A candle may be lit from the paschal candle and given as a sign of the share that the newly baptized has now been given in Christ's victory over death. Light not only signifies the glory of Christ (2 Corinthians 4:6) but also the reality that each Christian is called to be prepared to meet Him on the Last Day (Matthew 25:1–13). This candle can now be used during family devotions, or it can be lit during the celebration of future baptismal birthdays.

The newly baptized may be welcomed with the following:

A In Holy Baptism God the Father has made you a member / members of His Son, our Lord Jesus Christ, and an heir / heirs with us of all the treasures of heaven in the one holy Christian and apostolic Church. We receive you in Jesus' name as our brother(s)/ sister(s) in Christ, that together we might hear His Word, receive His gifts, and proclaim the praises of Him who called us out of darkness into His marvelous light.

**C Amen. We welcome you in the name of the Lord.**

## Welcome

In Baptism, the newly baptized has become a child of God and a member of God's family. As fellow members of that family, the congregation welcomes him or her as the newest of its members.

Stand

**P** Let us pray.
Almighty and most merciful God and Father,
we thank and praise You that You graciously preserve and enlarge Your family and have granted _name(s)_ the new birth in Holy Baptism and made _him/her/them_ _a member / members_ of Your Son, our Lord Jesus Christ, and _an heir / heirs_ of Your heavenly kingdom. We humbly implore You that, as _he/she/they_ _has/have_ now become Your _child/children_, You would keep _him/her/them_ in _his/her/their_ baptismal grace, that according to Your good pleasure _he/she/they_ may faithfully grow to lead a godly life to the praise and honor of Your holy name and finally, with all Your saints, obtain the promised inheritance in heaven; through Jesus Christ, our Lord.

**C** **Amen.**

**P** Peace ✠ be with you.

**C** **Amen.**

All return to their places.

## Prayer

A final prayer is offered for the newly baptized, that he or she might be kept living in his or her Baptism unto life everlasting.

# PART FOUR

## What you'll learn about:

- We are baptized into Christ's death and resurrection, forever binding us to Him.
- God sees our needs and gives us Absolution for our sins and His Holy Supper to nourish the faith planted by Baptism.
- God doesn't call His baptized children to lives of ease but to lives of total reliance on Him throughout trial and hardship.
- Though Baptism is a one-time event for each of us, its benefits are eternal and certain.
- Before time began, God chose us for adoption as His children.
- There is no greater comfort than knowing that "I am baptized" and that our salvation rests entirely in God's hands, not our own.

# What Does Baptism Mean for Me Now?

Baptism isn't just a memory of that moment water was splashed on us in church. It isn't a sign of our shoddy faith or faithfulness. It isn't even a singular gift that did its splendid work and called it a day. Rather, Baptism flows from the baptismal moment over the rest of our lives, granting grace, forgiveness, and familial benefits without end!

CHAPTER 7

# The Drowning That Gives Life

## In This Chapter

- Baptism unites us with Christ's death and resurrection.
- We need constant forgiveness, so God gives us Absolution.
- As God's family, we eat at His Table and receive His gifts.

**MAKING CONNECTIONS**

In the Lutheran baptismal rite, we renounce the devil, all his works, and all his ways. Then we state our Spirit-given belief in God the Father. In essence, the deed for our life is transferred from an abusive owner to a loving Father and Caretaker.

## A Reason for Rejoicing

There are dozens of reasons to rejoice in the gift of Holy Baptism. Baptism is the means by which God brings you into His own family. He grants you faith in Christ, and through that faith He delivers life, salvation, and forgiveness. He washes away all your sin and saves you from death and the devil. The list could go on and on.

As if that weren't enough, Paul speaks of the ongoing significance of Baptism in the Christian life. His writing shows how the benefits of Baptism are given anew each day through the gifts of Holy Absolution and the Lord's Supper.

## Baptism into Christ

In Paul's Letter to the Church at Rome, he makes it absolutely clear that the salvation they have in Christ is entirely a gift of God that they have not earned in any way. Paul lets his Jewish readers know that they are no more righteous than the Gentile Christians. He says, "All have sinned and fall short of the glory of God" (Romans 3:23). In the next chapter, he writes that the wicked are saved without having done anything to earn it: "And to the one who does not work but believes in Him who justifies the ungodly, his faith is counted as righteousness" (Romans 4:5).

By the time Paul gets to chapter 6, it seems as if there is no good reason to pay any attention to God's Law. Christians are saved completely apart from it. If the Law cannot condemn a Christian, why would a Christian want to keep it? But Paul doesn't stop there. He makes it even worse. It seems as if God likes forgiving sins so much that the best plan might be to work as hard as you can to sin so that God has even more wickedness to forgive!

Paul knows that his readers are going to be thinking those sorts of thoughts. He knows that the Gospel is going to sound too easy. Thus, he takes the time to teach the role of the Law in the life of a Christian by launching into an exposition of Holy Baptism. "What shall we say then? Are we to continue in sin that grace may abound? By no means! How can we who died to sin still live in it? Do you not know that all of us who have been baptized into Christ Jesus were baptized into His death? We were buried therefore with Him by baptism into death, in order that, just as Christ was raised from the dead by the glory of the Father, we too might walk in newness of life. For if we have been united with Him in a death like His, we shall certainly be united with Him in a resurrection like His" (Romans 6:1–5).

**WHAT DOES THIS MEAN?**

You have been absolved from sin and come to grace . . . in order to live a different life now and to abstain from sins. To be baptized and yet to remain in sin makes no sense. For Baptism is administered for the very purpose of taking away sin. (*WLS* § 153)

## Dead to Sin

The reason that Paul says we should not sin as much as we can is that we are dead to sin. How? We are baptized. Baptism, Paul argues, unites a person with Christ in His death and resurrection. When Jesus died on the cross to win forgiveness for all our sins, He destroyed sin's power to condemn. He emptied sin, death, and the devil of all their power. Paul says that when we are baptized, we are so closely united with Christ that the Lord's death is our death and the Lord's resurrection is our resurrection.

In Baptism we are dead to sin and alive in Christ. In the next few verses, Paul explores the implications of this: "We know that our old self was crucified with Him in order that the body of sin might be brought to nothing, so that we would no longer be enslaved to sin. For one who has died has been set free from sin. Now if we have died with Christ, we believe that we will also live with Him. We know that Christ, being raised from the dead, will never die again; death no longer has dominion over Him. For the death He died He died to sin, once for all, but the life He lives He lives to God. So you also must consider yourselves dead to sin and alive to God in Christ Jesus" (Romans 6:6–11).

**TECHNICAL STUFF**

Lutherans sometimes refer to the sinful nature as the "old Adam." The phrase translated "old self" in the ESV can also be translated as "old man." *Adam* is one of the most common words in the Old Testament to refer to humankind. The phrase "old Adam" also refers to the fact that the sin we are born with is inherited from Adam (Romans 5:12; Genesis 5:3).

## Die, Adam, Die

When Paul writes about the old self, he is talking about what Scripture elsewhere calls our "sinful nature." The sinful nature will always oppose God and His will. It will always try to drag us back into sin. This is why it is necessary for Baptism to kill the old Adam. After the old Adam is killed, the new person we are in Christ is free to "[live] to God."

In Baptism, what goes for Jesus goes also for us. Baptism gives us the enormous gift of being united with Christ in His life, death, and resurrection. God the Father regards us in the same way He does His own eternal Son. We are His precious child. We belong to Him.

However, another thing is clear from Romans 6. The old Adam doesn't die easily. Even though he is entirely defeated in the baptismal waters, we don't get to ignore the sinful nature in this life. This makes things very difficult. In order to survive, we need the Father's constant forgiveness.

**BELIEVE, TEACH, CONFESS**

In Baptism are given grace, the Spirit, and power to suppress the old man, so that the new man may come forth and become strong. (LC IV 76)

# The Father's Forgiveness

## Shouldn't This Be Simpler?

The baptismal life is tough. Since we are children of God and bear His name, it seems like life for the baptized should be easier than life is for those who have not been washed by water and the Word. Shouldn't the fact that we are so closely united with Christ in our Baptism mean that it's simpler to resist sin, love our neighbor, and live the Christian life?

It sure seems so. We want Baptism to make us more holy in a way that we can see in our day-to-day lives. We want Baptism to be *practical.* We want it to make it easier for us to obey Jesus when He says, "You therefore must be perfect, as your heavenly Father is perfect" (Matthew 5:48).

Sadly, Baptism doesn't make things easier. If anything, Baptism makes things harder. Baptism unites us with Christ, and that has implications that we'd rather not think about. Once we are united with Christ in Baptism, we should expect the world to treat us the same way it treated Him.

## This Is Your Life

Jesus has a lot to say about how the life of one of His baptized disciples will look. He says, "If anyone would come after Me, let him deny himself and take up his cross and follow Me" (Matthew 16:24). The life of the baptized Christian is going to be filled with suffering. Our Lord's Baptism led Him to the cross, and we should not expect our lives to be any different. Jesus also says, "If the world hates you, know that it has hated Me before it hated you" (John 15:18).

The problem that baptized Christians face in their earthly lives is that our sinful flesh doesn't want to let us go. Christians have two minds. We have the new mind that Christ has given us in Baptism. This mind wants only to do what the Lord commands. It never even considers sin. It always does good from a willing and joyful spirit. But our old sinful nature never wants to let go. It holds on for dear life and drags us back into the mire over and over again.

## Oops! I Did It Again!

If you are like most Christians, you probably have a few sins that you struggle with more than others. It's not that you don't know they're sins. You fully realize that these actions are evil and that Christians should not

**MAKING CONNECTIONS**

Forgiveness needs to be a constant part of the Christian life, and with God it is. He delights in forgiving us over and over again. It is not this way with sinful man. At one point, Peter was trying to get Jesus to put a limit on the forgiveness he was expected to give. Jesus refused. His answer amounted to "Stop counting."

"Then Peter came up and said to Him, 'Lord, how often will my brother sin against me, and I forgive him? As many as seven times?' Jesus said to him, 'I do not say to you seven times, but seventy-seven times.' " (Matthew 18:21–22)

**FROM THE BIBLE**

For I know that nothing good dwells in me, that is, in my flesh. For I have the desire to do what is right, but not the ability to carry it out. For I do not do the good I want, but the evil I do not want is what I keep on doing. (Romans 7:18–19)

behave in such a way. When you commit one of these sins, you probably pray, "I've done it again! God, forgive me! I hate it when I behave this way. Please give me strength to do better!" After you ask for the Lord's forgiveness, things might get better for a while. You might think, "I've finally made progress in my battle with this sin." But sooner or later, you fall again. You are disgusted with yourself and hate the fact that you can't seem to overcome the sins that plague you.

In a comment on Romans 6, Luther acknowledged all of this. "The sooner a person dies after baptism, the sooner is his baptism completed. For sin never ceases entirely while the body lives, which is so wholly conceived in sin that sin is its very nature, as the prophet says, 'Behold I was conceived in sin, and in iniquity did my mother bear me.' There is no help for the sinful nature unless it dies and is destroyed with all its sin. Therefore the life of a Christian, from baptism to the grave, is nothing else than the beginning of a blessed death. For at the Last Day God will make him altogether new" (AE 35:31).

**FROM THE BIBLE**

Be kind to one another, tenderhearted, forgiving one another, as God in Christ forgave you. (Ephesians 4:32)

## Absolutely Absolved

There is only one thing that can sustain a baptized Christian during the ongoing struggle of earthly life. A Christian needs to continually receive the forgiveness of sins. One of the ways God loves to deliver that forgiveness is through the gift of Holy Absolution.

Jesus instituted the gift of Holy Absolution on the day of His resurrection. "Jesus said to them again, 'Peace be with you. As the Father has sent Me, even so I am sending you.' And when He had said this, He breathed on them and said to them, 'Receive the Holy Spirit. If you forgive the sins of any, they are forgiven them; if you withhold forgiveness from any, it is withheld' " (John 20:21–23).

God knows how difficult life is for the baptized. He knows the struggle that we daily face. He doesn't want us to fall into despair because of our daily addiction to sin. Instead, God wants us to always have a way to hear about and receive the forgiveness that Christ has won for us on the cross.

## Time to 'Fess Up

Because of our need for forgiveness, God gives the gift of Absolution. Absolution can come to us in several different ways. If we sin against a friend or a family member, we can ask for their forgiveness personally. When that forgiveness is given, it is sure and certain. Paul writes, "Put on then, as God's chosen ones, holy and beloved, compassionate hearts, kindness, humility, meekness, and patience, bearing with one

**BELIEVE, TEACH, CONFESS**

Speaking of Baptism and the third Sacrament (Absolution), Luther says, "Baptism, both in its power and meaning, includes also the third Sacrament, which has been called repentance. It is really nothing other than Baptism. What else is repentance but a serious attack on the old man <,that his lusts be restrained,> and an entering into a new life? Therefore, if you live in repentance, you walk in Baptism" (LC IV 74–75).

another and, if one has a complaint against another, forgiving each other; as the Lord has forgiven you, so you also must forgive" (Colossians 3:12–13).

Sometimes we may not feel comfortable confessing our sin to the one we hurt. Sometimes this may not even be possible because of the nature of the sin. That is why God has given authority to the pastoral office to forgive sins. This is done publicly in the Divine Service for all the sins we commit. However, for particularly troubling sins, private Absolution is also available. When you go to your pastor and ask him to forgive your sins, you don't need to worry about embarrassing him. Most pastors have heard many confessions, and it's very unlikely that the sin that is bothering you is going to be the most shameful sin that he's heard—and even if it is, he will forgive you nonetheless!

God has given you your pastor so that your sins can be forgiven in a sure and certain way. God wants you to hear it. God doesn't just forgive your sin in general, He forgives the particular sin that is bothering you. When your pastor hears your confession, he will forgive whatever it is you confess. He will tell you that Christ has taken *that* sin to the cross. He will tell you that *your* transgression has been atoned for. What particular sin it is doesn't matter. You can't come up with a sin so bad that your pastor will not absolve it. That's because Christ's blood covers it. Your pastor will proclaim to you what God has already said in your Baptism: You are forgiven. You are free.

## Run for Your Life

Luther describes the gift of Absolution in this way: "If you were a Christian, then you ought to be happy to run more than a hundred miles to Confession. . . . You should rather come and compel us to give you the opportunity. For in this matter the compulsion must be the other way around: we must act under orders, you must come into freedom. We pressure no one, but we let ourselves be pressured, just as we let people compel us to preach and to administer the Sacrament" (BEC 30–31).

Your pastor wants to deliver Christ's forgiveness to you. God guarantees that forgiveness in the promises He makes to you in your Baptism. Demand it. Force your pastor's hand. Don't let a day pass of unnecessarily carrying the burden of your sins on your back. Jesus wants to take them away, and that's why He's given you your pastor.

**TECHNICAL STUFF**

God gives the Sacraments to His people for their forgiveness, life, and salvation, and this happens as they call upon Him in trust and with confidence in Christ, the Savior. By the sixteenth century, the Roman Church had developed a complicated sacramental system that had transformed the Sacraments into meritorious works performed by priests. This was especially evident in the Mass, where priests "sacrificed" Christ again and again on behalf of the living and the dead. The Bible, however, reveals the key to the Sacraments: the promises of God. God attaches His Word of promise to the element of the Sacrament—water, wine, or bread—and gives and strengthens the faith of those receiving them. (*Lutheranism 101*, p. 136)

**MAKING CONNECTIONS**

Baptized Christians are the royal priesthood of the Most High God. The priesthood is permanent. Once God claims us, it is for good. Psalm 110:4 is reminiscent of this: "The LORD has sworn and will not change His mind, 'You are a priest forever after the order of Melchizedek.' "

Remember that in Baptism, you have a new Father, one who has adopted you into His own holy family. You are a son or daughter of God. Your Father doesn't want you to hide your face from Him in shame. He doesn't want you to shield yourself with leaves and hide from Him in the garden. He loves you. He wants to forgive you. You are precious to Him. That is the joy of Baptism that makes the struggle bearable. That is the joy of Baptism that daily forgiveness sustains.

## Eating Together

Baptism brings you into God's family. You are His adopted child, an heir of eternal life. God the Father freely gives you what you do not deserve. He treats you as if you are the firstborn as He invites you to His Table.

The family that forgives lives. That's why the Father wants to make sure that you always have access to His absolutely sure and certain word of forgiveness. That's why the Father makes sure that you can always receive comfort when your sins afflict you. Forgiving children is what fathers do. There is nothing that can make a truly loving father hate his child. There is nothing that you can do to make God the Father revoke your status as His adopted child.

## Come and Get It

That's why God the Father invites you to Supper. He knows that you need to hear that your specific sins are forgiven, and so He gives you Absolution. But He also knows that children need to eat. He knows that it is the Father's responsibility to feed His children. It is for this reason that God has established His Holy Supper. God isn't miserly with His gifts. He wants to feed you in abundance.

The Lord's Supper is God's way of feeding His baptized children. Remember that Jesus is the Lamb of God who takes away the sin of the world. He is the Passover Lamb who shed His holy blood on the cross so that all of God's family might be spared from God's just judgment against their sins.

The Passover meal did not take place in the tabernacle or the temple. It was a family meal instituted before either of those places existed. As the fulfillment of the Passover, the Lord's Supper is also a family meal, one that is shared among the members of God's family.

**FROM THE BIBLE**

Blessed are those who are invited to the marriage supper of the Lamb. (Revelation 19:9)

**MAKING CONNECTIONS**

When faith speaks, it prays. Jesus gave us the Lord's Prayer in response to His disciples' plea of "teach us how to pray." It is the family prayer of the Christian Church. In Holy Baptism, your child is made a child of God. Now he or she is privileged to call God "Father." (Fast and Fast, p. 24)

## Sharing Supper

Through Jesus' words, His own body and blood are offered and received in the Lord's Supper. We eat the body and drink the blood of the Lamb who was slain. In this meal, God joins us together into one holy family. Because Christ's body and blood are in all of those who receive the Sacrament, they are united and strengthened in the faith that Christ gave in their Baptism.

Our life together as God's family shares much in common with our lives in our earthly families. Studies have repeatedly shown that regularly shared family meals are one of the best ways to equip children for success and strengthen familial bonds. Simply put, families that eat together stay together. They share their triumphs and griefs. They rejoice in the provision that God has made for them. They thank the cook for preparing the meal. As a family, they take joy in one another's company. All the while, though, they are being strengthened for when they must part.

When we eat the Lord's Supper together, the same sorts of things are happening. The members of the Body of Christ are united in joy and in suffering by receiving into their mouths the true body and blood of Christ. As the baptized, we share one another's burdens. We rejoice when our brothers rejoice. We mourn when our sisters mourn.

## Tidings of Comfort and Joy

Luther describes the joy of the meal in this way: "Whoever is in despair, distressed by a sin-stricken conscience or terrified by death or carrying some other burden upon his heart, if he would be rid of them all, let him go joyfully to the sacrament of the altar and lay down his woe in the midst of the community [of saints] and seek help from the entire company of the spiritual body—just as a citizen whose property has suffered damage or misfortune at the hands of his enemies makes complaint to his town council and fellow citizens and asks them for help. The immeasurable grace and mercy of God are given us in this sacrament to the end that we might put from us all misery and tribulation [*anfechtung*] and lay it upon the community [of saints], and especially on Christ. Then we may with joy find strength and comfort, and say, 'Though I am a sinner and have fallen, though this or that misfortune has befallen me, nevertheless I will go to the sacrament to receive a sign from God that I have on my side Christ's righteousness, life, and sufferings, with all holy angels and the blessed in heaven and all pious men on earth' " (AE 35:53–54).

**FROM THE BIBLE**

If one member suffers, all suffer together; if one member is honored, all rejoice together. (1 Corinthians 12:26)

# Study Questions

1. What is the image that Paul uses for Baptism in Romans 6?

2. What is the role of Holy Absolution in the life of the baptized Christian?

3. What is the role of the Lord's Supper in the life of the baptized Christian?

*Visit lutheranism101.com to download the free Leader Guide.*

# Discussion Questions

1. Private Confession and Absolution is unquestionably one of the most underutilized blessings in the modern Lutheran Church. While it is not required for anyone, what benefits may individual Christians be missing out on by not taking advantage of this opportunity? How could wider use affect the culture of an entire congregation or church body?

2. How is life for the baptized Christian different from life for one who is not baptized?

*Visit lutheranism101.com to download the free Leader Guide.*

PUTTING IT ALL TOGETHER

# Baptism As Exorcism

Another way that Lutherans talk about Baptism is as an exorcism, the driving out of an unclean spirit, the devil himself, from the soul of the baptized. This is Luther's use of exorcism in Baptism in his *The Little Book of Baptism* (1526). Traditionally, it directly followed the Flood Prayer. That Luther retained the exorcism as part of his baptismal order became a major issue between Lutherans and the Swiss reformers who followed Calvin. Lutherans contended that it was necessary to retain the exorcism to counter the Pelagian threat of the Anabaptists and the Calvinists. The Reformed theologians denounced it as, at best, an unnecessary remnant of Roman Catholic liturgy and, worse, of papal magic. Luther and the Lutherans rejected the rationalistic belief that the devil was simply a biblical metaphor; rather, they firmly believed in the reality and personality of the devil and the Church's continual struggle against him. The theological importance of the baptismal exorcism is described by Dr. Scaer: "Exorcism is an answer to synergism, since here God alone acts to release the believer from Satan's grip. Not only is the use of the exorcism in Baptism a statement of the awareness of the supernatural power of Satan and evil, it is also a complete rejection of human righteousness" (Scaer, p. 184). One form or another of Luther's exorcism was retained in many Lutheran baptismal liturgies until late in the twentieth century.

"Therefore, thou miserable devil, acknowledge thy judgment and give glory to the true and living God, give glory to his Son Jesus Christ and to the Holy Ghost, and depart from this [*name*], his servant; for God and our Lord Jesus Christ has of his goodness called him to his holy grace and blessing, and to the fountain of baptisms so that thou mayest never dare to disturb this sign of the holy cross ☩ which we make on his forehead; through him who cometh again to judge, etc.

So hearken now, thou miserable devil, adjured by the name of the eternal God and of our Savior Jesus Christ, and depart trembling and groaning, conquered together with thy hatred, so that thou shalt have nothing to do with the servant of God who now seeks that which is heavenly and renounces thee and thy world, and shall live in blessed immortality. Give glory therefore now to the Holy Ghost who cometh and descendeth from the loftiest castle of heaven in order to destroy thy deceit and treachery, and having cleansed the heart with the divine fountain, to make it ready, a holy temple and dwelling of God, so that this servant of God, freed from all guilt of former sin, may always give thanks to the eternal God and praise his name forever and ever. Amen."

CHAPTER 8

# The Christian's Identity and Daily Comfort

## In This Chapter

- Though a one-time event, Baptism's benefits are eternal.
- There is no surer comfort than knowing "I am baptized."
- Baptism is entirely God's work, not ours.
- We were predestined for adoption as God's children.

## Baptism's Eternal Benefits

God's Word says so much about the gift of Baptism! You have great cause to be filled with wonder and gratitude that God favors us with such a precious gift. Luther once wrote, "Every Christian has enough in Baptism to learn and to do all his life. For he has always enough to do by believing firmly what Baptism promises and brings: victory over death and the devil, forgiveness of sin, God's grace, the entire Christ, and the Holy Spirit with His gifts" (LC IV 41).

Baptism has enduring significance for you. You can rejoice in the phrase "I am baptized" as you consider what it says about your eternal relationship with Jesus, your Savior. You may have had only a few hours, days, or weeks of life before you received the gift of Baptism. You may have received the gift much more recently and have vivid memories of it. Maybe the day of your Baptism is still coming.

Whatever your situation, there is one crucial thing you must remember: even though the act of Baptism takes only a few seconds, its benefits are eternal.

# I Am Baptized

## A "Good" Person

When I was in grade school, I would often spend a week each summer with my aunt, uncle, and cousins in Missoula, Montana. One summer, I went to visit my cousins during the week of the Missoula County Fair. This trip was especially exciting because my cousins lived only a few blocks from the fairgrounds, and we could come and go as we pleased.

One day at the fairgrounds, my cousin Grant and I were walking past a line of booths that were selling arts and crafts. At the end of the line was a booth sponsored by a local church. A man from this booth approached me. He wanted to ask me what he said would be "the most important question of my life." Even though I didn't really want to talk to him, I agreed to listen.

The question was simple, but it took me by surprise. He asked, "If you were to die tonight, why would you go to heaven?" In those years, I was a typical kid when it came to church. I complained constantly. I tried to avoid going to church any way that I could think of. I told my parents that all they did in Sunday School was talk about Jesus. (I thought that was a great argument, but it really just meant that I had great Sunday School teachers.) Because of all this, I gave a lousy reply to the man's question. I said, "I'm a good person."

**FROM THE BIBLE**

You did not choose Me, but I chose you and appointed you that you should go and bear fruit and that your fruit should abide. (John 15:16)

## Becoming a Christian

My answer was completely wrong. I'm not a good person and never have been. I'm a sinner. I deserve eternal hell and condemnation. The answer I gave would have gotten me nowhere with Jesus, and it also got me nowhere with the man from the church booth. He told me that Jesus suffered and died on the cross to forgive my sins and that if I accepted Jesus as my Savior, I'd live forever with Him in heaven. That sounded very similar to what I'd heard in church, so I said, "That's what I believe."

At this point, the man became very excited. He thought that I'd just accepted Jesus into my heart right there on the spot. He asked me to pray a special prayer, wrote the time and date on a card, and gave it to me. He said that I now knew the exact moment that I'd become a Christian. He encouraged me to find a church where they taught what he'd told me. I was confused by that because I was pretty sure I already went to a church like that.

As sincere and earnest as the man was, he was also wrong. I did not become a Christian at the Missoula County Fairgrounds during a summer in the early 1980s. I had actually become a Christian at Our Redeemer Lutheran Church in Columbia Falls, Montana, on a Sunday morning in May 1973. I was just a few weeks old when it happened. I had become a Christian when I'd been baptized. As misguided as the man was, he was right about one thing: I did know the exact moment I'd become a Christian. I'd actually known it my whole life.

**MAKING CONNECTIONS**

In Baptism we now put on Christ—
Our shame is fully covered
With all that He once sacrificed
And freely for us suffered.
For here the flood of His own blood
Now makes us holy, right, and good
Before our heav'nly Father.
(*LSB* 596:4)

## A Good Answer and a Great One

When we were approached by the people from the booth at the fair, my cousin Grant gave a far better answer than I did. He said that he believed that Jesus had suffered and died on the cross to forgive all his sins. This was very true, and it was a better answer than I had given! But was it the best answer? No. Not exactly.

Though what Grant had said was accurate in every detail, it was not the most sure and certain answer that he could have given. Jesus did indeed suffer and die to win forgiveness for all of Grant's sins. Grant did indeed believe that. By the grace of God, Grant still believes it. But the best answer that Grant or I could have given would have also been the most simple and straightforward one. Each of us should have said, "I am baptized."

## Blessed Assurance

The reason that Baptism provides us with the strongest and most certain assurance of salvation should be obvious by now. Baptism is God's action for us. If we say, as Grant did, that we *believe* that Jesus has suffered and died to forgive all of our sins, we open the door of uncertainty just a crack. Grant didn't realize he was introducing an element of doubt any more than I realized I was taking credit for my salvation, but that is what was happening.

When we focus on Baptism, we are focusing on the fact that God has adopted us, made us His own children, and washed away all of our sins. We are holding onto something that is outside of ourselves. God's promises do not change. Malachi makes this plain when he gives us these words of God: "I the LORD do not change; therefore you, O children of Jacob, are not consumed" (Malachi 3:6). God will never go back on the commitment He makes to us in Baptism. We need not ever worry about how God regards us when we become His baptized children. The only thing that could separate us from God's promise would be if we were to reject all of the gifts He offers by abandoning the faith He has given. Faith receives the gifts of Baptism. If we throw away the gift of faith, all of the other gifts are lost as well. This couldn't be more different from the reality we confess in the sentence "I am baptized." When we say this, we are holding firmly onto what *God* is doing. And the joy of it is this: God has eternally committed Himself. He's not going to change his mind.

**FROM THE BIBLE**

Reproaches have broken my heart, so that I am in despair. I looked for pity, but there was none, and for comforters, but I found none. (Psalm 69:20)

## From the Mountains to the Valleys

Over the course of any ordinary Christian's life, personal awareness of his or her faith in Jesus will wax and wane. There will be moments—perhaps after a hymn, a great sermon, or a fun retreat—when we will feel like we've summited a mountain in our faith life. For a time, we might be frequently aware of the peace we have in Christ or even weep tears of joy. Those moments are great, and we should thank God for them. But we must never base our faith *on* them.

Between one mountaintop and the next, there will always be a valley, and sometimes those valleys will be very deep. When we're on the mountain, we might think, "See, I know because of the way I feel that I have sure, certain, and indestructible faith in Jesus as my Savior," but this would only set us up for serious doubts when we descend into the valley. When suffering enters our lives, we will think, "Well, I'm not so sure of my faith now. Things are pretty bad. I'm struggling. I wonder if Jesus still loves me?" These and many other doubts can assail us. Satan will see these doubts as weaknesses that he can exploit, and he will attack us vigorously. He will try to drive us from uncertainty to despair.

## Along for the Ride

It is a perfectly wonderful thing for us to say that we believe that Jesus died on the cross to forgive all of our sins. Indeed, the only place Christians find true certainty of salvation is in Christ's work on the cross. However, there's a more tangible and personal answer to the question, if you were to die tonight, why would you go to heaven? A question that important needs an answer that is completely certain. It needs an answer that is objectively true regardless of how we might feel at the moment. It needs one like "I am baptized."

When you say "I am baptized," you are not placing yourself in the driver's seat. God's got it covered. You're along for the ride—passive. You are on the receiving end of what's happening, getting what God is giving. He is doing all that is needful for your salvation. You have nothing to worry about and nothing to do.

## What Do You Say?

To say "I am baptized" is a source of comfort, because in those three words, you are summarizing all that Scripture says about Baptism. You are saying that God has put His name on you and claimed you as His own. You are saying that He has made you a disciple. You are saying that He has given you faith in Christ. You say all this, and so much more!

With joy, you are saying that He has adopted you as His own child by giving you new birth. With a peaceful heart, you are saying that you've received the gift of the Holy Spirit. With utter certainty, you are saying that He has drowned your old Adam and given you new life in Christ.

**FROM THE BIBLE**

For by grace you have been saved through faith. And this is not your own doing; it is the gift of God, not a result of works, so that no one may boast. (Ephesians 2:8–9)

## In His Hands

You are not the active one in any of those sentences. You are the one receiving the benefits of God's action for you on the cross and in Baptism. If anyone asks you why you'll go to heaven, you want to give them an answer that is completely sure and completely certain. You want to tell them that God has saved you. You want to tell them that you are *baptized*!

But if you are ever in that situation and say that you are baptized, your answer probably won't satisfy the person you're talking to. They will think you are trusting in something that you did. They will think that you are saying that you're saved because you obeyed God's command. But you know the answers to those objections. You know that it was God who saved you in your Baptism. You know that He is the one who washed all your sins away. You know that by saying you're baptized, you're leaving your salvation entirely in God's hands. You've got some wonderful news that you can share, and who knows? Maybe the guy at the fair booth can begin to rejoice in his Baptism as much as you rejoice in yours!

## Holy Election

By now, you have more than enough reason to rejoice in your Baptism. God promises to give so many gifts through those holy waters. Indeed, what a precious thing it is to be able to say, "I am baptized!" But there's still more.

In Ephesians 1:4–6, Paul writes, "In love He predestined us for adoption as sons through Jesus Christ, according to the purpose of His will, to the praise of His glorious grace, with which He has blessed us in the Beloved." The Scriptures teach that before even the foundation of the world was laid, God determined in His great love and mercy to save us. In eternity, before time began, God chose every Christian to be His own.

Paul ties God's eternal election of His Church to Baptism. He says that God predestined us "for adoption as sons through Jesus Christ." Adoption! The gift of being God's children! New birth through water and the Word! You know what Paul is talking about. This is all Baptism talk.

**FROM THE BIBLE**

And we know that for those who love God all things work together for good, for those who are called according to His purpose. For those whom He foreknew He also predestined to be conformed to the image of His Son, in order that He might be the firstborn among many brothers. And those whom He predestined He also called, and those whom He called He also justified, and those whom He justified He also glorified. (Romans 8:28–30)

### Fighting the Monster

The fact that God has elected us to be His own children is something that should give us joy and comfort, but the monster of uncertainty loves to enter into our minds with all sorts of doubts. The monster asks, "How do you know you are one of the elect? How do you know that it was the purpose of God's will to save *you*? What makes you so sure that God wants you with Him forever in heaven?" The answer to all of these questions could not be more simple.

I am baptized!

In Baptism, God has revealed His gracious will toward you. In Baptism, God has adopted you as His own child. In Baptism, God has said, "You are My own child! I love you! My love for you extends backward to the time before I created time! My love for you extends forward into all eternity! You are precious to Me! I will never let you go!"

### Perfectly Provided

The Formula of Concord in the Lutheran Confessions puts it this way: "God was greatly concerned about the conversion, righteousness, and salvation of every Christian. He so faithfully ‹provided for it› that even before the foundation of the world was laid, He considered it, and in His purpose ordained how He would bring me to salvation and preserve me in salvation" (FC SD XI 45).

It would be hard to imagine anything that fits this description of God's provision better than Baptism. Baptism reveals in time what God has intended for you from eternity. Baptism gives to you in the here and now what God has always wanted you to have. There are no ifs, ands, or buts about it. Baptism is the kind of gift that we could never imagine ourselves.

## Most Certain! Most True!

All that is left is to rejoice. All that is left is to sing the praises of the God who has loved us in this way. Let's conclude by considering these words of Luther:

"[Every Christian] has always enough to do by believing firmly what Baptism promises and brings: victory over death and the devil, forgiveness of sin, God's grace, the entire Christ, and the Holy Spirit with His gifts. In short, Baptism is so far beyond us that if timid nature could realize this, it might well doubt whether it could be true. Think about it. Imagine there was a doctor somewhere who understood the art of saving people from death or, even though they died, could restore them quickly to life so that they would afterward live forever. Oh, how the world would pour in money like snow and rain. No one could find access to him because of the throng of the rich! But here in Baptism there is freely brought to everyone's door such a treasure and medicine that it utterly destroys death and preserves all people alive.

"We must think this way about Baptism and make it profitable for ourselves. So when our sins and conscience oppress us, we strengthen ourselves and take comfort and say, 'Nevertheless, I am baptized. And if I am baptized, it is promised to me that I shall be saved and have eternal life, both in soul and body' " (LC IV 41–44).

This is most certainly true.

# Is Your Destiny Written?

In Matthew 25, Jesus uses a picture of a shepherd separating sheep and goats to describe His final judgment of all people on the day of His return. In the parable, the sheep are those who had faith in Him, and the goats are those who expected to be saved through their own righteousness. If we read Jesus' words in this parable carefully, we learn something very important about the nature of divine election.

Jesus says to the sheep, "Come, you who are blessed by My Father, inherit the kingdom prepared for you from the foundation of the world" (Matthew 25:34). Jesus tells the sheep that their reward was prepared for them before He even created the world. They were eternally chosen to have faith in Him, receive the forgiveness of sins, and live a resurrected life of perfect joy and peace for all eternity.

When we say that in Baptism, God reveals His good will toward us, this is exactly what we're talking about. God chose to claim us as His own before He created us. The doctrine of election comforts us because it tells us that God chose us for salvation in Christ before He even created the earth, the sun, or the stars.

For some Christians, there is a tragic flip side to this teaching. Among these are the Reformed who believe that if some are elected for eternal salvation, then all others must be elected for eternal damnation. They would say that if you want to read the Scriptures in a logical and consistent way, you must believe that from eternity, God has elected all people for heaven or hell.

The words of Jesus are a great help! To the goats, He says, "Depart from me, you cursed, into the eternal fire prepared for the devil and his angels" (Matthew 25:41). Do you notice the difference? Jesus told the sheep that heaven had been prepared for them "from the foundation of the world." On the other hand, the goats are headed for a place that was "prepared for the devil and his angels." Jesus plainly teaches that the sheep are going where He has always intended them to go. The goats are going somewhere that wasn't intended for them at all.

**NEED TO KNOW**

In Reformed Calvinistic theology, the doctrine that all events have been willed by God is sometimes called "double predestination" because they teach that God actively chooses (elects) those who will go to heaven *and* those who will go to hell.

There are many places in the Scriptures where God could teach election to damnation if He wanted to, but He never does. Not once. What does this mean for us? It means that when you read the passages in the Scriptures that deal with election, you can remember that God has given those passages for your comfort. You can also remember that in Baptism, God has adopted you as His own child, and He is never going to take back what He said in those waters.

# Study Questions

1. Is there a difference between saying "I am baptized" and saying "I believe in Jesus"?

2. Where is the only place that Christians can truly find certainty of their salvation?

3. What is the relationship between Holy Baptism and election?

*Visit lutheranism101.com to download the free Leader Guide.*

# Discussion Questions

1. We are told to always be prepared to defend our faith (1 Peter 3:15). What are the ways in which we prepare to do this?

   Regardless of how much we prepare, what's the most important factor in our defense of the faith?

2. Some people might be pretty shocked if you said, "I am baptized!" when they asked, "If you were to die tonight, why would you go to heaven?" What are some objections they might raise, and what would be a good way to answer them?

   a. I know lots of people who are baptized that don't believe in Jesus.

   b. How can you say that you're saved by something you do? That's works righteousness!

3. How can Baptism give comfort when life is difficult?

PUTTING IT ALL TOGETHER

# Baptism Abides Forever!

## By Martin Luther

Baptism is not a short-term blessing. Nor is it something we ever need to do more than once. It is a one-time, for-all-time gift through which God works daily and eternally. Luther says it well, so he'll have the last word (from LC IV 77–83):

> Our Baptism abides forever. Even though someone should fall from Baptism and sin, still we always have access to it. So we may subdue the old man again. But we do not need to be sprinkled with water again [Ezekiel 36:25–26; Hebrews 10:22]. Even if we were put under the water a hundred times, it would still be only one Baptism, even though the work and sign continue and remain. Repentance, therefore, is nothing other than a return and approach to Baptism. We repeat and do what we began before, but abandoned.
>
> I say this lest we fall into the opinion in which we were stuck for a long time. We were imagining that our Baptism is something past, which we can no longer use after we have fallen again into sin. The reason for this is that Baptism is regarded as only based on the outward act once performed ‹and completed›. This arose from the fact that St. Jerome wrote that "repentance is the second plank by which we must swim forth and cross over the water after the ship is broken, on which we step and are carried across when we come into the Christian Church." By this teaching Baptism's use has been abolished so that it can no longer profit us. Therefore, Jerome's statement is not correct, or at any rate is not rightly understood. For the ship of Baptism never breaks, because (as we have said) it is God's ordinance and not our work [1 Peter 3:20–22]. But it does happen, indeed, that we slip and fall out of the ship. Yet if anyone falls out, let him see to it that he swims up and clings to the ship until he comes into it again and lives in it, as he had done before.
>
> In this way one sees what a great, excellent thing Baptism is. It delivers us from the devil's jaws and makes us God's own. It suppresses and takes away sin and then daily strengthens the new man. It is working and always continues working until we pass from this estate of misery to eternal glory.

# Prayers

## Of a Sponsor

Dear Lord Jesus, I thank You for the honor of being a sponsor for (*name*). You have brought (*name*) into Your kingdom through the washing of water and Your Word, and You have forgiven all his (her) sins. Since Your Holy Spirit has given (*name*) faith in Your for life and salvation, help me to be a good example of Christian faith and life for him (her), so that he (she) may learn to observe everything that You have commanded. Help (*name*) to learn from Your Word of truth that You love him (her) with an everlasting love. Help him (her) to learn the Ten Commandments, the Apostles' Creed, and the Lord's Prayer. Help him (her) to attend the services of Your house, hear Your life-giving Word, and learn to sing Your praises. Please keep (*name*) faithful to You and bring him (her) one day to Your Table, where You will strengthen his (her) faith as he (she) eats and drinks Your own body and blood in Holy Communion. Please keep (*name*) faithful to You and Your Church throughout his (her) life, and finally bring him (her) to Your eternal wedding feast. In Your holy name I pray. Amen.

## Of a Parent

Lord Jesus, when parents brought their children to You so that You could touch them and bless them, You said, "Let the little children come to Me" (Matthew 19:14). I thank You for giving (*name*) to me to raise according to Your Word and for bringing him (her) to Yourself through the waters of Holy Baptism. Thank You for forgiving all of his (her) sins, for rescuing him (her) from death and the devil, and for giving him (her) eternal life as You promise in Your Word. I thank You for touching my son (daughter) through the washing of water and Your Word. Please bless me, and give me wisdom to teach (*name*) Your Word of truth and life, and help him (her) to learn the joys of Your forgiveness. Help him (her) to learn the Ten Commandments, the Apostles' Creed, and the Lord's Prayer. When I bring (*name*) to Your house, help him (her) to learn how much You love him (her), and help (*name*) to love and worship You, Your heavenly Father, and the Holy Spirit. Please strengthen the faith of (*name*), and bring him (her) one day to Your Table, where he (she) will eat and drink Your body and blood in Communion and receive Your forgiveness, life, and salvation. Amen.

# Glossary

**Absolution.** Literally, "set free." This Latin term was used by theologians as a translation of the biblical word *aphiemi*, "to set free, cancel, or forgive."

**absolve.** To set free from sin. By virtue of his office, in the name and stead of Christ, a pastor forgives those who have confessed their sins, affirmed their faith in Christ, and promised to amend their lives (Matthew 16:19; 18:18; John 20:19–23).

**altar.** A stone or wooden structure at the center of the chancel from which the Lord's Supper is celebrated; the sacramental focus from which God gives His gifts; the sacrificial focus of the congregation's worship.

**Amen.** Hebrew word meaning "it is true; reliable."

**Baptism.** From the Greek word meaning "to bathe" or "to wash." Many religions have religious washings. But Christian Baptism applies water "in the name of the Father and of the Son and of the Holy Spirit" as described by Jesus (Matthew 28:19). In Baptism, God washes away the person's sins and welcomes that person as a member of His kingdom. Through water joined to God's Word, the Holy Spirit puts to death our sinful nature, connects us to Christ in His death and resurrection, and gives us new spiritual birth as God's children.

**baptismal shell.** Either a real shell or made of precious metal, the baptismal shell is used to apply water in Holy Baptism. Much early Christian artwork depicts Baptism using a cup or shell. For example at Jesus' Baptism, He is shown standing in the river and John is using a shell to scoop water and baptize Jesus.

**baptistery.** A church building built specifically for baptisms. Most of these ancient structures had eight sides to confess the new birth we receive in Baptism.

**blessing.** A showering of divine favor; anything good that God gives His people.

**burnt offering.** A form of sacrifice in the Old Testament in which the entire body of an animal was burned. In this way, the whole animal was offered to God.

**circumcision.** The surgical removal of the foreskin from a boy's or man's penis.

**Communion, Holy.** "Communion" or "participation" translates the Greek word for fellowship, *koinonia*. To take part in something, to share something. In the Lord's Supper, communicants partake of the body and blood of Christ and are made members of His Body, the Church (1 Corinthians 10:16–17). Another name for the Sacrament of the Altar; *see* Sacrament of the Altar.

**confession.** The act by which one admits or confesses sin(s) and the guilt of sin.

**disciple.** A follower or student of a teacher, leader, or master. In the New Testament, often used to refer to those who followed Jesus.

**divine passive.** A grammatical construction in the Scriptures denoting the voice of verbs in which the subject undergoes the action of the verb and where the One performing the action (while often not named) is understood to be God Himself.

**Divine Service.** The service of Word and Sacrament that is the chief weekly service of the parish. The setting in which God serves those present with Word and Sacrament; only of secondary importance is our service to God, our worship.

**election.** The doctrine that before even the foundation of the world was laid, God determined in His great love and mercy to save us in Christ Jesus.

**elements.** The visible materials used in the Sacraments. In Baptism, the element is water. In Holy Communion, the elements are bread and wine.

**font.** Large basin or pool that holds water for Holy Baptism.

**God's Word.** The Holy Scriptures; the inspired revelation of God's plan and record of salvation.

**Gospel.** The message of Christ's death and resurrection for the forgiveness of sins, eternal life, and salvation. The Holy Spirit works through the Gospel in Word and Sacrament to create and sustain faith and to empower good works. The Gospel is found in both the Old and New Testaments.

**Holy Spirit baptism.** The teaching among some Christians that the Holy Spirit is given apart from the water Baptism that Christ instituted in Matthew 28:19.

**Invocation.** From the Latin for "call upon"; the words "In the name of the Father and of the Son and of the Holy Spirit" spoken at the beginning of the service; serves as a reminder of Holy Baptism.

**Israelite.** A descendant of Jacob, son of Isaac. Because Jacob was also called Israel, his descendants are often called Israelites.

**liturgy.** In its broad and most basic sense, liturgy equals **Divine Service**, in which God gathers His people around Word and Sacrament and serves His gifts to them. More narrowly, the liturgy is the words, music, and order for the celebration of the Divine Service, particularly as the Church has handed it down over the centuries.

**Lord's Prayer.** The model prayer Jesus taught to the disciples (Matthew 6:9–13). Sometimes it is called the Our Father, after the first words of the prayer.

**Lord's Supper.** Another name for the Sacrament of the Altar; *see* Sacrament of the Altar.

**Means of Grace.** The means by which God gives us the forgiveness, life, and salvation won by the death and resurrection of Christ: the Gospel, Absolution, Baptism, and the Lord's Supper.

**office.** A specific authority entrusted to specifically chosen people to do specific functions. For example, the Office of the Holy Ministry is the authority to preach, teach, and administer the Sacraments.

**original sin.** The state into which human beings are born because of the sin they inherit from Adam in consequence of the fall.

**pastor.** Latin for "shepherd"; the title for the congregation's public minister who is ordained and called to be the spiritual supervisor of the "flock" that gathers around Word and Sacrament to receive God's good gifts.

**Pietism.** As a movement within Lutheranism, it started in the seventeenth century; it emphasized personal piety and personal spiritual improvement over doctrinal correctness. It saw biblical doctrine as less important than "a religion of the heart."

**piscina.** A special sink in a church building with a drain that goes directly into the ground instead of a septic or sewage system. It is used solely to dispose of sacramental elements (wine from the Lord's Supper or water from Holy Baptism) in a reverent way.

**Rationalism.** A philosophical movement that determines what is true on the basis of human reason rather than Holy Scripture.

**regeneration.** From a Latin word meaning "rebirth." The Holy Spirit gives new life through Baptism and God's Word.

**repentance.** The turning away from sin toward faith in Christ and His sacrifice for us.

**sacrament.** From the Greek word meaning "mystery"; literally, "something sacred." In the Lutheran Church, a Sacrament is a sacred act that (1) was instituted by God, (2) has a visible element, and (3) offers the forgiveness of sins earned by Christ. The Sacraments include Baptism, the Lord's Supper, and also Absolution (if one counts the pastor as the visible element; Large Catechism IV 74; Apology XIII 4–5).

**Sacrament of the Altar.** Sacrament by which the Lord offers His body and blood under the form of consecrated bread and wine for Christians to eat and drink; through such eating and drinking, communicants receive the gifts of the forgiveness of sins and the strengthening of faith; also called Holy Communion, the Eucharist, and the Lord's Supper.

**Sanhedrin.** The highest court of justice and the supreme council in Judaism. The Great Sanhedrin was led by the high priest and met in the temple in Jerusalem. The Great Sanhedrin handed Jesus over to Pontius Pilate to be crucified. At least two members of the Sanhedrin (Nicodemus and Joseph of Arimathea) may have objected because they believed that Jesus was the Messiah.

**sin.** Betraying God; rejecting His will and His ways; any thought, word, or deed that departs from the will of God.

**sinful nature.** Our human nature, after the fall, is thoroughly corrupted by sin, making us God's enemies and lovers of ourselves.

**speaking in tongues.** The supposed supernatural ability to speak in heavenly languages. In the New Testament, every example of speaking in tongues refers to speaking a human language. Some Christians today believe that this ability is a sign or confirmation that one has received the gift of the Holy Spirit.

**Table of the Lord.** Another name for the Sacrament of the Altar; also a term for the altar itself. *See* Sacrament of the Altar.

**testament.** A will that establishes the disposition of one's belongings at the time of death, or a covenant established by God between God and man. The Lord's Supper fulfills both definitions: prior to the cross, Jesus leaves Christians His body and blood for the forgiveness of their sins; and this Sacrament is part of His covenant of grace for man.

**Trinity, triune.** One true God in three persons: Father, Son, and Holy Spirit.

**unity.** The spiritual bond all Christians share with one another as a gift from God because of their faith in Christ.

**worship.** The service to which God calls and gathers His people to give to them the gifts of life and salvation by means of Word and Sacrament.

**Yahweh.** God's name. The Hebrew language originally did not have vowels. God's name is written "YHWH." However, we know how God's name is pronounced because of the way it is written when combined with other words like *Hallelujah* and because of the way it was transposed into Greek in the ancient world.

9780758634085